SpringerWienNewYork

EDITION architektur.aktuell 05
Matthias Boeckl (Ed.)

Wien | Vienna
New Urban Architecture

Springer Wien New York

Univ.-Prof. Dr. M. Boeckl,
SpringerWienNewYork
Sachsenplatz 4–6
1201 Wien

© 2005 Springer-Verlag/Wien
Printed in Austria

SpringerWienNewYork is a part of Springer Science+Business Media
springeronline.com

Coverabbildung unter Verwendung eines Photos von Paul Ott

Redaktion | Editorial Team: Andrea Nussbaum, Gerald A. Rödler
Übersetzung | Translation: J. Roderick O'Donovan
Grafik | Graphic Design: A | H Haller
Druck | Printing: Grasl Druck & Neue Medien, A-2540 Bad Vöslau

Gedruckt auf säurefreiem, chlorfrei gebleichtem Papier – TCF
Printed on acid-free and chlorine-free bleached paper

SPIN: 11404750

Bibliografische Information Der Deutschen Bibliothek
Die Deutsche Bibliothek verzeichnet diese Publikation in der
Deutschen Nationalbibliografie; detaillierte bibliografische Daten sind im Internet
über <http://dnb.ddb.de> abrufbar.

Mit zahlreichen (großteils farbigen) Abbildungen

ISBN-10   3-211-25249-5 SpringerWienNewYork
ISBN-13   978-3-211-25249-9 SpringerWienNewYork

INHALT | CONTENTS

Wien-Donaucity

Sechzehn Jahre nach der Wende, die übrigens unweit Wiens an der Grenze zwischen Österreich und Ungarn ihren Ausgang nahm, haben sich heute die Nebel der Geschichte gelichtet. Was in der ersten Euphorie nach der Implosion der sozialistischen Regime Osteuropas wie eine erneute Wiener Hauptstadtchance auf supranationaler Ebene aussah, das wurde inzwischen einer anderen, kaum weniger viel versprechenden Realität angepasst. Die kontinentale Megalopolis-Vision wich einem realen Alltag, der nach über sechzig Jahren Trennung endlich wieder Normalität in die Beziehungen zwischen Wien und seinen unmittelbaren Nachbarn brachte. Von der Lage in einer europäischen Sackgasse ist Wien abrupt wieder ins Zentrum des südöstlichen Mitteleuropa gerückt, dessen Brennpunkt es einst Jahrhunderte lang war. Die problematische Vision einer restaurativen Blüte Wiens durch regionale Dominanz und massiven Zuzug ist aber nun glücklicherweise der intensiven wirtschaftlichen und kulturellen Kooperation zwischen gleichberechtigten Partnern gewichen. Dass die gesamte österreichische Ostregion, aber auch die angrenzenden Regionen Tschechiens, Ungarns, Sloweniens und der Slowakei davon in jeder Hinsicht massiv profitieren, ist unbestritten. Für Wien als einzige Millionenstadt zwischen Belgrad und Prag, zwischen Budapest und München wäre alles andere wohl auch unnatürlich.

Dieses Buch bietet einen Querschnitt durch die wichtigsten Architektur- und Städtebaufragen, mit denen Wien in dieser ersten Phase einer neuen europäischen Normalität konfrontiert ist – und es zeigt durchwegs anspruchsvolle Lösungen, die dabei entstehen. Naturgemäß geht es dabei vor allem um Anpassungs- und Positionierungsfragen. Denn sowohl strukturell als auch inhaltlich hat Wien derzeit eine singuläre historische Chance, seine überregionale Rolle selbst zu definieren und zu nutzen. Dazu wird im nachfolgenden Interview mit Planungsstadtrat Schicker recht deutlich, was Wien kann und bei welchen Rollenbildern es geringere Chancen im globalen Städtewettbewerb hat. Für die Architektur ergeben sich daraus Schwerpunkte bei der Infrastruktur, bei Corporate Headquarters, beim Kongresstourismus, bei Bauten für Kultur, Bildung und Wissenschaft sowie beim Dauerthema des Bestandsumbaus. Im Zusammenspiel zwischen den neuen Nutzungen der historischen Kernstadt und den neuen Verkehrs-, Büro- und Forschungsfunktionen rundum entstehen beachtliche Energien eines starken urbanen Kraftfeldes. Und auch eine Menge Know-How, das Wien verstärkt exportieren könnte. Klar wird aber auch, dass der Umbau viel zu langsam vonstatten geht, dass durch die mangelhafte Infrastruktur bei Bahn und Straße, durch die viel zu spät in Angriff genommene Nachrüstung und Verbindung mit dem Osten viel Zeit im galoppierenden Strukturwandel ungenutzt verstrichen und für die Stadtentwicklung verloren ist. In diesem Sinne sollte dieses Buch auch als kleiner Beitrag zur Stadtbeschleunigung wirken. Je mehr Projekte jenes Qualitätsniveaus entstehen, wie es auf den folgenden Seiten anhand rezenter Baubeispiele präsentiert wird, desto größer ist Wiens Gewicht als Kompetenzzentrum für Integration von Geschichte und Zukunft – und zwar in ideeller und materieller Hinsicht.

Sixteen years after the major political changes in Europe, which, incidentally, began not far from Vienna along the border between Austria and Hungary, the mists of history have now cleared somewhat. What seemed in the initial euphoria following the implosion of the socialist regimes in Eastern Europe to be a renewed chance for Vienna to emerge as a capital city on the supranational scene, has in the meantime been adapted to a different but hardly less promising reality. The vision of a continental megalopolis has given way to an everyday reality that, after sixty years of separation, has reintroduced normality into the relationships between Vienna and its immediate neighbours. From being in a European cul-de-sac Vienna has suddenly been shifted to the centre of southeastern Europe, a region where for centuries it formed the focus. The problematic vision of a restorative blossoming of Vienna through regional dominance and massive immigration has thankfully made way for intense economic and cultural collaboration between partners of equal status. It is undeniable that the entire eastern region of Austria, but also the adjoining regions of the Czech Republic, Hungary, Slovenia and Slovakia are profiting massively from this development in every respect. For Vienna, as the only city with a population of over a million between Belgrade and Prague and between Budapest and Munich, anything else would be most unnatural.

This book offers a cross-section through the most important questions of architecture and urban planning now confronting Vienna in the first phase of this new European normality – and it presents a number of thoroughly ambitious solutions that are in the process of developing. Naturally, the main focus is on questions of adaptation and positioning. Both structurally and in terms of content Vienna has at present a unique opportunity to itself define and utilize its own supra-regional role. The interview with Rudolf Schicker, City Councillor for Urban Development, Traffic and Transport, makes quite clear what Vienna can do, while also outlining those roles in which Vienna's chances in the global competition between cities are less than excellent. For architecture the outcome is a focus on the areas of infrastructure, corporate headquarters, convention tourism, buildings for culture, education and science as well as the perennial theme of converting the existing substance. In the interplay between new uses for the historic core city and the new transport, office and research functions considerable amounts of energy are released in a strong urban field of forces. And also a large amount of know-how that Vienna can increasingly export. However, it is also made clear that the conversion is being carried out far too slowly and that, due to inadequacies in the rail and road infrastructure, to the excessive delay in retrofitting and developing connections to the east a lot of valuable time was wasted that has been lost for the process of urban development. In this sense this book is intended as a small contribution to urban acceleration. The more projects completed at the level of quality demonstrated by the recent examples presented on the following pages, the greater Vienna's weight as a competence centre for the integration of history and the future will be – in both the ideal and material respects.

Matthias Boeckl

Wien, der urbane Brennpunkt Mitteleuropas
Vienna, the Urban Focus of Central Europe

Rudolf Schicker, Stadtrat für Stadtentwicklung und Verkehr,
im Gespräch mit Matthias Boeckl und Robert Temel

Rudolf Schicker, Executive City Councillor for Urban
Development, Traffic and Transport,
in interview with Matthias Boeckl and Robert Temel

Stadtrat Rudolf Schicker
PHOTO PETRA SPIOLA

Wien steht im europäischen Städtewettbewerb und will dort ein wichtiger Player sein. Wie könnten wir uns da positionieren?
Es gibt Städte, die einen großen Vorteil haben – nämlich Hauptstädte von großen Staaten zu sein. Und die noch dazu aus der Kolonialzeit und aus der Ära des frühen Kapitalismus Positionen einnehmen, die für wesentliche Wirtschaftszweige Messen, Börsen und Umschlagplätze sowie Stützpunkte für Banknetzwerke und Ähnliches gebracht haben. Diese Bedeutung hat Wien nicht mehr. Es macht keinen Sinn, sich mit solchen Städten ernsthaft im Wettbewerb messen zu wollen, da man dabei höchstens kleine Erfolge ernten könnte. Wo wir aber große Vorteile haben: Wir sind Hauptstadt eines Mitgliedslandes der Europäischen Union und wir haben eine große Vergangenheit aus der Zeit eines ehemals viel größeren Staatsgebietes. Das erste gehört zur aktuellen Politik, das zweite ermöglicht uns, aus der Geschichte, aus der historischen Bedeutung der Stadt, für den Tourismus, in der Kultur, in der Kunst, in der Musik viele Vorteile zu ziehen. In der weltweiten Positionierung geht es uns als Eineinhalb-Millionen-Stadt wesentlich besser als „normalen" Eineinhalb-Millionen-Städten, denn Hauptstädte haben es grundsätzlich leichter.
Es geht uns auch deshalb besser, weil wir in der Neuzeit die Welthauptstadt der Musik waren und es, so hoffe ich, immer noch sind. Diese Dinge beiseite zu schieben und zu sagen: Mozart ist schon zweihundert Jahre tot, Strauß schon über hundert Jahre, warum also geben wir uns damit ab – das wäre falsch. Musik ist nach wie vor eine wichtige Trademark für Wien und wir können uns damit für Neues positionieren. Aber wir müssen dabei das Neue auch nützen. Wir sollen uns der Bedeutung der Geschichtsträchtigkeit dieser Stadt sehr bewusst sein, aber wir dürfen darin nicht ersticken. Daher brauchen wir den Freiraum für neue Architektur, den Freiraum für neue Musik, etwa elektronische Musik, wo das auch gelungen ist: wir haben eines der besten Dokumentationszentren auch auf diesem Gebiet. Wir exportieren aus dieser Stadt jede Menge Architektur. Und wir können auch innerhalb der Stadt noch ausreichend Spielraum für moderne Architektur bieten. Wir sind auch sicher mit dem Bereich Stadt- und Umwelttechnologien führend. Wien ist eine „reiche" Stadt – reich in Bezug auf das BIP pro Kopf, nicht beim Kommunalbudget, das immer zu wenig ist. Wien ist bei allen EU-Berechnungen stets die fünft- oder sechsreichste Region Europas, und daher können wir uns im Umweltbereich vieles leisten – ob das nun Kanalisation, Kläranlagen oder Müllentsorgungseinrichtungen sind –, was sich andere Städte (noch) nicht leisten können oder wollen. Dieser Schwerpunkt bringt uns Vorteile.

Vienna is engaged in the competition between the different European cities and wants to be a major player. How can we best position ourselves?
There are certain cities that have an enormous advantage, namely the capital cities of large countries. In addition, thanks to their history as centres of colonial empires and their expansion during the era of early capitalism they still enjoy a position in several important areas of the economy that is reflected by their trade fairs, stock exchanges, trading centres, hubs for banking networks etc. Vienna no longer has this kind of importance. There is no sense in trying to compete with these cities – the most we could hope for would be minor victories. But we have major advantages: we are a capital city of a member country of the European Union and we have a glorious past dating from the time when Vienna was the capital of a far larger country. The former is an element in the current political situation, the latter historical fact helps us derive numerous advantages from our history, from the historic importance of the city in the field of culture, the arts in general and music in particular. As a city with a population of one and a half million we are in a far better position in the worldwide rankings than "normal" cities of this size, because, essentially, things are easier for capital cities.
Things are easier for us also because in the modern period Vienna was the world capital of music and still is, or at least I hope so. To shove these things aside and say: "Mozart has been dead for two hundred years, Strauß for more than a hundred, why bother still pushing this kind of thing?" would be very wrong. Music remains an important trademark for Vienna and one that we can use to position the city in a new way. But we must also utilize new aspects. We should be extremely conscious of this city's great historic past but we should not let it suffocate us. Therefore we need space for new architecture and for new music, for example electronic music, where we have had some measure of success. In this field we boast one of the best documentation centres. We export quite an amount of architecture from this city. Vienna is a "wealthy" city, rich as regards the GDP per head of the population, but not in terms of the communal budget that is always too small. In the EU tables and listings Vienna is always the fifth or sixth richest region of Europe and therefore we can afford a great deal in the area of the environment – whether it be drainage, sewage treatment plants or garbage disposal facilities – that other cities cannot (yet) afford or do not want to afford. This focal point gives us certain advantages.

Boris Podrecca
IMP3, Biotech-cluster

Beste Öko-Infrastruktur und Wohnsituation, Zukunftsfeld Wissenschaft

Wir haben in Wien eines der besten öffentlichen Verkehrssysteme, wir können bei Stadttechnologien international mithalten und können das auch verwerten, etwa bei Breitband-Glasfaserkabelverlegungen im Kanal, beim Sauberhalten der Kanäle durch Roboter und Ähnlichem. Da gibt es einiges, das kaum bekannt ist, da es auf Kommunen spezialisiert ist. Das können wir verwerten und da sollten wir auch weitermachen. Wir sind auch bekannt als Stadt, die seit der Zwischenkriegszeit im Wohnbau in der Lage ist, die Grundversorgung zu gewährleisten, sehr niedrige Miethöhen zu haben und trotzdem in der Qualität des Wohnbaus und der Architektur immer wieder Neues zu bieten – jüngst fand etwa die Grundsteinlegung des Projekts 9=12 statt.

Wir sollten also diesen speziellen Mix kultivieren. Was nicht ganz zu Wien passt, ist zum Beispiel ein Weltruf als Standort Olympischer Spiele. Da wäre die Nachnutzung wahrscheinlich zu gering, da sind die Wienerinnen und Wiener zuwenig in der Breite der verschiedensten Sportarten aktiv.

Wien war jedoch in der Zwischenkriegszeit ein Ort wissenschaftlicher Höhepunkte, in den Geisteswissenschaften, in den Naturwissenschaften und in der Medizin. Wir hatten einige Nobelpreisträger, die ab 1938 vertrieben, aber nach 1945 als „unsere" Nobelpreisträger reklamiert wurden. Besser wäre es gewesen, sie nach dem Krieg zurückzuholen. Wir haben aber in letzter Zeit wieder eine positive Entwicklung, die man verstärken muss. Wir haben an den Universitäten mit Zeilinger, mit Penninger und Schröder einige zurückgeholt, die im naturwissenschaftlichen Bereich hervorragende Arbeit leisten. Wir haben mit dem AKH eine medizinische Universität, die weltweit einen hervorragenden Ruf hat. Mit dem IMP beginnend, ist in St. Marx ein *Biotechnologiecluster* entstanden. Und wir haben im Automotive-Bereich – Thema Windkanal und alles, was sich dort rundherum ansiedelt – einen weiteren Schwerpunkt. Das sollte man nicht klein reden, es gehört aber noch sehr stark gepflegt, damit wir wieder den früheren Wissenschafts-Standard erreichen, auch in den Geisteswissenschaften.

Best ECO-Infrastructure and Housing, Science as the Area of the Future

In Vienna we have one of the best public transport systems, in the field of urban technology we can compete at an international level and can also utilize our competence in this area, which includes laying broadband-glass fibre cables in drains, cleaning drains by means of robots etc. There are things that are not widely known, as their application at communal level is so specialised. We are utilizing our knowledge in this area and we should continue to do so. We also have a reputation as a city that, ever since the interwar period, has been able to meet essential needs in the area of housing at very low rents and that repeatedly offers something new in terms of the quality of its housing and architecture. Very recently, for example, the foundation stone of the project 9=12 was laid. We must cultivate this special mix. But it would be inappropriate for Vienna to aim for a worldwide reputation as host location for the Olympics. The use of the facilities after the Games would probably be too slight and there are too few Viennese active in the various different sports.

But in the interwar period in Vienna highpoints were reached in various scientific fields, in the natural sciences and in the area of medicine. We had a number of Nobel prize-winners who were forced to emigrate in 1938 only to be reclaimed after 1945 as "our" Nobel prize-winners. A better idea would have been to encourage them to return after the war. But in more recent times we have had a positive development that should be strengthened. With Zeilinger, Penninger and Schröder at our universities we have brought back a number of people who are carrying out exceptional work in the area of natural sciences. In our General Hospital (AKH) we have a medical university that enjoys an excellent worldwide reputation. The IMP in St Marx represents a start in establishing a *biotechnology cluster*, and we also have the area of automotive engineering – the wind tunnel and everything to do with it – as a further focal point. This should not be played down but should be given strong support so that we can reach the standards of earlier days, in the field of humanities also.

Wie sieht die Positionierung Wiens in Bezug auf die östlichen Nachbarn aus?

Unsere Region ist das südliche Zentraleuropa. Dieser Begriff vermeidet Konflikte mit der Achse Berlin-Warschau-Baltikum-Russland, wo wir sicher nicht mitspielen können. Ein großer Schwerpunkt kann im südlichen Zentraleuropa von Prag über Krakau, Brünn, Bratislava bis Budapest, sowie der gesamte Balkan bis Istanbul und Athen für uns liegen.

Bis Istanbul?

Ja, ganz bewusst. Ich rechne zwar nicht mit einem baldigen EU-Beitritt der Türkei, aber Istanbul ist eine europäische Stadt.

Stadtpolitisch spielt der EU-Status also keine Rolle?

Nein, wir brauchen die guten Kontakte auch mit Zürich, mit Belgrad, mit Zagreb, wir haben sie zur Zeit bereits sehr intensiv mit Sofia und Bukarest. Wir können und dürfen uns nicht nur auf die Europäische Union einschränken lassen. Und wir erzielen mit dieser Stadt-Außenpolitik sehr gute Resultate. Wien ist glaubwürdig in seiner Bemühung um die Partnerstädte, da wir sie nicht dominieren wollen. Das ist für Wien leicht, denn aus einem Acht-Millionen-Staat heraus kann man niemanden dominieren. Für Berlin ist es schwieriger, denn aus einem 80-Millionen-Staat kann man schon ganz gern wirtschaftlich dominieren wollen. Wir haben in der Kooperation vieles anzubieten und wir wissen auch um die Qualitäten der Kollegenschaft in diesem Städten. Ein Beispiel ist Belgrad, wo jeder sagen wird, was hat Wien damit zu tun und warum kümmern die sich darum? Die Antwort: Erstens liegt Belgrad an der Donau, zweitens gibt es in Belgrad nicht nur dumpfe Nationalisten, sondern zum Beispiel auch eine Verkehrsfakultät an der Universität, die schon in den 1960er Jahren mit Wien hervorragende Kooperationen hatte. Belgrad hat damals genauso wie Wien seine U-Bahn geplant – wir haben sie nun, in Belgrad ist es jedoch nicht dazu gekommen.

Städtekooperationen:
Beispiel Istanbul und Bratislava

Und wir haben zum Beispiel auch in Istanbul mit Ausnahme der U-Bahn die Situation, dass alles, was auf Schienen fährt, aus Floridsdorf geliefert wurde, entweder von SGP oder von Bombardier. Die Istanbuler Experten wurden in Wien ausgebildet und sprechen perfekt Deutsch. Solche Entwicklungen müssen wir einfach nutzen, das sind die großen Vorteile, die diese Stadt wirtschaftlich hat. Im kleineren Radius ist es die entscheidende Frage, wie stark es uns gelingt, aus den notgedrungen bestehenden Konkurrenzsituationen in einer Region Vorteile zu ziehen und nicht nur die Nachteile zu bejammern. Wir werden die Konkurrenz zwischen Wien und Bratislava nicht wegbekommen, auch nicht zwischen Wien, Prag und Budapest. Aber wir können von den Vorteilen einer großen Region profitieren.

Schätzen sie diese Konkurrenz etwa zu Bratislava derzeit als hochgradig ein?

Wir schätzen sie nicht so ein, aber wir bemerken, dass die Kollegen und Freunde in Bratislava uns so einschätzen, nämlich dass wir ihnen zu sehr sagen wollen, wo es lang geht. Und dass wir das Potential, das sie bieten, nach Wien absaugen (könnten). Diese Gefahren bestehen aber gegenseitig. Wir erleben ja, wie locker es niederösterreichischen Politikern von den Lippen kommt, von der „Vienna Region" zu sprechen, wenn es um Standortpolitik geht. Offensichtlich kann man mit Wien besser werben als mit Niederösterreich. Daran ist auch nichts auszusetzen, wir profitieren in dieser Region alle davon. Bratislava vollzieht einen raschen Aufholprozess, in welchem die Vorteile von Kooperation noch nicht so klar auf der Hand liegen. Auf

What about Vienna's position in relation to the city's eastern neighbours?

Our region is southern central Europe. This term neatly avoids conflicts with the axis Berlin-Warsaw-Baltic States-Russia where we certainly cannot compete. A major focus for us could lie in southern central Europe, from Prague via Cracow, Brno, Bratislava to Budapest as well as to the entire Balkan area and as far as Istanbul and Athens.

As far as Istanbul?

Yes I say this quite deliberately. Although I don't believe that Turkey will join the EU, in the near future, Istanbul is nevertheless a European city.

Does this mean that, in terms of urban politics, EU status does not play a role?

That is correct. We also need to maintain good contacts with Zurich, Belgrade, and Zagreb. At the moment have particularly intensive contacts with Sofia and Bucharest. We cannot (nor ought we) restrict ourselves to the European Union. And our urban foreign policy is achieving excellent results. Vienna's efforts to establish relationships with partner cities are well received, as we have no wish to attempt to dominate anyone. This is easy enough for Vienna; a country with only eight million inhabitants cannot attempt to dominate anyone. For Berlin things are more difficult because a country with a population of 80 million may well be seen as wanting to dominate. We can offer a great deal in terms of cooperation and we are also aware of the qualities of our colleagues in these cities. One example is Belgrade where most people would say: "what business does Vienna have there and why is it involved there?" The answer is, firstly, that Belgrade is on the Danube and, secondly, the city is not inhabited solely by inveterate nationalists. There is also a traffic and transport faculty at the university that cooperated with Vienna at a high level as early as the 1960s. At that time Belgrade was planning an Underground system, just like Vienna, the difference being that we have one now, whereas in Belgrade they don't, yet.

Cooperation between Cities:
Istanbul and Bratislava as Examples

And, for example, we have the situation in Istanbul where everything that runs on tracks – apart from the Underground – was supplied from Floridsdorf, from either the SGP or Bombardier companies. The Istanbul experts were trained in Vienna and speak perfect German. We must utilize such developments; these are the major economic advantages that Vienna has. At a smaller scale the decisive question is how successful we can be in using the competitive situation forced upon us to our advantage, rather than complaining about the disadvantages. We will not be able to eliminate the competition between Vienna and Bratislava, nor between Vienna, Prague and Budapest. But we can profit from the advantages of a larger region.

Do you see the competition with Bratislava as particularly intense?

We ourselves don't see it this way but we do notice that colleagues and friends in Bratislava maintain that we always want to tell them how to do things, and that we (could) divert the potential that they offer towards Vienna. But this danger exists on both sides. At present, for instance, we note the casual way in which politicians from Lower Austria speak of the Vienna Region when discussing matters of business location. Seemingly Vienna is a far more effective advertising medium than Lower Austria. We don't object to this, all of

lange Sicht verlieren aber beide Seiten. Daher schlagen wir vor, in Kooperation zu arbeiten, die Vorteile zu nutzen, die der Automotive-Cluster in der Slowakei bietet, wie unser GM-Werk und unser Windkanal im Norden Wiens zum Beispiel.

Gibt es da bereits konkrete Kooperationsprojekte zwischen den Automotive-Unternehmen Wiens und der Slowakei?
Ob die Unternehmen selber das schon planen, weiß ich nicht. Wir würden es jedenfalls sehr unterstützen und Sie haben vielleicht schon davon gehört, dass wir im Bereich der Ausbildung von ArbeitnehmerInnen bereits Kooperationen mit der Region Bratislava eingegangen sind. Wir haben die Situation Flughafen Wien-Schwechat und Flughafen Bratislava. Alle wissen, dass der Flughafen Bratislava privatisiert werden soll, alle schauen erwartungsvoll in Richtung mögliche Ausschreibung des Verkaufs. Die Gefahren für die Region sind größer, wenn wir zwei konkurrierende Flughäfen in 50 Kilometer Distanz haben, als eine Kopperation der beiden Flughäfen, wo für beide Städte mehr herauszuholen ist.

Das ist realistischerweise nur durch gegenseitige Beteiligungen möglich. Denkt die Stadt Wien daran, Anteile am Flughafen Bratislava zu erwerben?
Es spricht nichts dagegen, hier eine Verschränkung zustande zu bringen.

Welche weiteren Anbindungsprojekte befinden sich derzeit bereits „auf Schiene" oder Straße?
Auf dem Sektor Straße wurde der Bau der A 5 bereits begonnen, so dass Kittsee und Bratislava verbunden werden. Dann gibt es eine durchgehende Autobahnverbindung, das ist Standard, der herzustellen ist, das ist keine Frage, ob man es aus Umweltgründen gerne sieht oder nicht, aber europäische Hauptstädte sind im Straßennetz eben mit Autobahnen verbunden. Wir werden dasselbe Richtung Norden benötigen, dort ist die Nordautobahn notwendig, sie soll, allerdings erst später, gebaut werden.

**Schlüsselprojekt Zentralbahnhof Wien –
und eine neue Schiffsverbindung**
Was den Schienenverkehr betrifft, so glaube ich, dass uns mit der Entscheidung für den Zentralbahnhof Wien Europa Mitte ein ganz großer Schritt gelungen ist. Wir können damit auch erstmals sichtbar machen, dass sich Wien nicht mehr als große Haupt-, Reichs- und Residenzstadt fühlt, wo alle nur *hin*fahren wollen und einen Kopfbahnhof benötigen. Wir befinden uns im Netzwerk der Städte und wollen einen Knotenpunkt bieten, über den man von Norden nach Süden, von Osten nach Westen und in alle anderen Himmelsrichtungen fahren kann, ohne dass man aus dem Zug steigen und mit der Straßenbahnlinie 18 von einem Bahnhof zum anderen wechseln muss. Alles das lässt sich mit diesem neuen Durchgangsbahnhof bewerkstelligen. Und er hat zusätzlich den Vorteil, dass der Flughafen Wien in die Fernverbindungen eingebunden werden kann. Der zweite Punkt einer rezenten Vereinbarung zwischen Bürgermeister Häupl und Vizekanzler Gorbach zu diesem Thema ist, dass nicht nur der Bahnhof Wien Europa Mitte sehr rasch kommen soll, sondern dass auch am Flughafen die notwendigen Vorkehrungen getroffen werden, und dann die Schienenverbindung vom Flughafen zur Ostbahn der Fischa entlang gebaut wird.

Ist das eine komplett neue Trassierung?
Ja. Sie ist nicht lang, nur ca. 13 km, aber damit erreichen wir, dass die Fernzüge von Budapest und Bratislava, von Linz und St. Pölten direkt zum Flughafen geführt werden können. Damit vergrößert sich der Radius für den Flughafen enorm. Das ist der Fernverkehr. Im Nahverkehr gibt es das Angebot der Stadt

us in the region profit. Bratislava is catching up rapidly and in the present situation perhaps the advantages of cooperation are not so obvious. But in the long term both sides suffer from this kind of attitude. Therefore we suggest working cooperatively, exploiting the advantages that the automotive engineering cluster in Slovakia offers, or our GM Works and our wind tunnel in the north of Vienna, for example.

Are there already concrete cooperation projects between the car-manufacturing businesses in Vienna and in Slovakia?
Whether the companies themselves have plans in this direction I cannot say. We would certainly support this kind of cooperation – perhaps you have heard that we have already started to collaborate with the Bratislava region in the area of worker training. We have Vienna International Airport in Schwechat and Bratislava airport. Everyone knows that Bratislava airport is going to be privatised and everybody is looking forward to the announcement of the sale. The danger for the region when there are two competing airports within 50 kilometres from each other is far greater than when the two cooperate – which would, in any case, offer both cities far more.

But realistically speaking this is only possible if both sides are willing to cooperate. Is the City of Vienna interested in acquiring shares in Bratislava airport?
There would be no objections on our side to such a move.

What other such projects are presently "on track" or indeed "on the road"?
Regarding road building: construction of the A 5, which will connect Kittsee and Bratislava, has already started. There will be then a continuous motorway connection and this is the standard that must be reached, whether one has reservations about it for environmental reasons or not. The fact simply is that European capitals are connected by a network of motorways. We will need the same kind of connection to the north, we need to construct the Nordautobahn (north motorway) but it will only be built later.

The Key Project: A new Central Railway Station for Vienna – and A new Boat Connection
As far as rail traffic is concerned I think that the decision to erect a new central railway station – Wien Europa Mitte – represents a major step forward. For the first time we can demonstrate clearly that Vienna no longer sees itself in its former role as an imperial capital city and royal residence which, as it was the *final* destination for everyone only needed terminus stations. Today we are part of a *network* of cities and we want to form a node through which people can travel from north to south and from east to west and in every other direction without having to change trains or to travel with the 18 tram from one main railway station to the other (as is the case at the present). A new central railway station that trains can travel through will make this possible. And it will offer the additional advantage of integrating Vienna International Airport in the intercity rail network. The second point of a recent agreement between vice-chancellor Gorbach and Mayor Häupl was not only that a rapid start should be made with the construction of the new station (Wien Europa Mitte) but that the requisite construction measures should be implemented at Vienna airport and a rail connection from the airport to the Ostbahn (Eastern Line) should be built along the River Fischa.

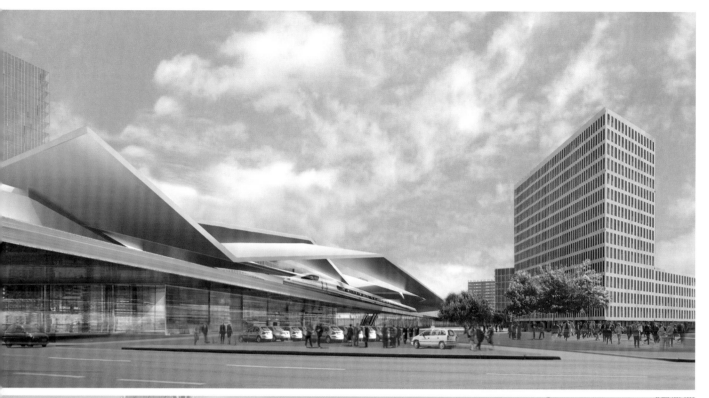

Albert Wimmer/Hotz-Hoffmann
Masterplan, urban development Wien-Europa-Mitte

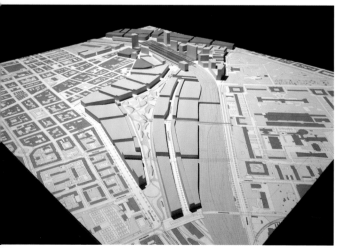

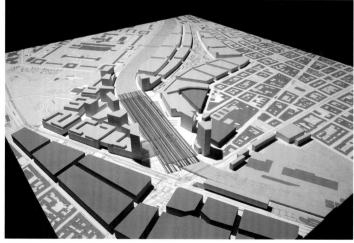

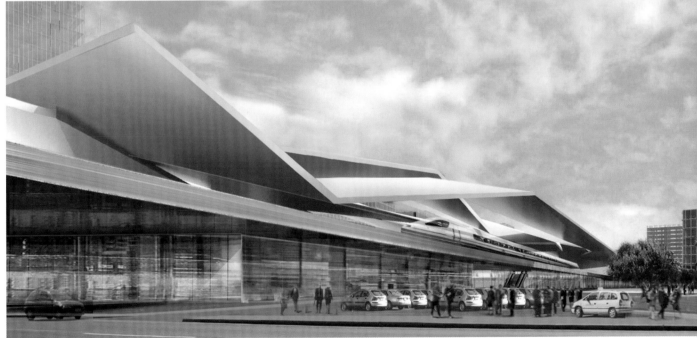

Albert Wimmer/Hotz-Hoffmann
Halle des Bahnhofs Wien-Europa-Mitte zwischen zwei Bürotürmen
New railway station between office towers

Wien und des Bürgermeisters, dass der City Air Train (CAT) nach Bratislava verlängert wird und auch dort den Flughafen künftig einbinden soll. Das ist aber etwas schwierig, weil dort keine Bahnstrecke unmittelbar vorbeiführt.

Das heißt, man müsste auch dort eine neue Bahnstrecke bauen. Wie weit ist das Projekt dieser Bahnverlängerung nach Bratislava in den Gesprächen mit der Slowakei gediehen und sind auch von dieser Seite Investitionen geplant?
Die sind meines Wissens noch nicht ganz so weit, wir werden aber eine Möglichkeit ohne große Nachteile für die Benützer schaffen können. Wir können ja den CAT über die Schienen der alten Pressburger Bahn bis Wolfsthal verlängern, und von dort könnte man mit einem Bus problemlos die Verbindung zum Flughafen Bratislava herstellen.

Da müsste man aber umsteigen.
Ja, aber es gibt noch die Gleistrasse, die sich wiederherstellen lässt. Der Grund ist im Besitz der Gemeinde Wolfsthal und wäre für die Bundesbahn wieder rückkaufbar. Es gibt aber ein weiteres interessantes Projekt zwischen Wien und Bratislava, das mir besonders gefällt, weil es eine Innovation für beide Städte ist: Nämlich von Stadtzentrum zu Stadtzentrum mit dem Schiff zu fahren. Alle Schiffsverbindungen waren bisher so, dass man zum Handelskai fahren musste und von der Reichsbrücke abgefahren ist. Der Mexikoplatz hat einen entsprechenden Ruf und ist nicht wirklich attraktiv.

Dann wird es der Schwedenplatz sein?
Genau, um den geht es dabei. Es soll der Schwedenplatz sein und damit die Möglichkeit geboten werden, vom Stadtzentrum Wien flussabwärts in weniger als einer Stunde unmittelbar zur Innenstadt von Bratislava zu fahren. Retour bräuchte es ein wenig länger, aber Richtung Bratislava wäre man sogar schneller als mit dem Zug.

Gibt es dazu bereits Studien?
Es wird untersucht. Dabei es geht nur um die Frage, ob man einen Bedarfs- oder einen Linienbetrieb einrichtet, also ein oder zwei Schiffe einsetzt mit Tagesrandverbindungen. Ich finde es sensationell, dass wir damit Wien und Bratislava auch mit dem Schiff verbinden und zeigen können, dass es zwischen diesen beiden Städten etwas sehr Spannendes gibt, nämlich das grüne Herz der Region, den Nationalpark, der jedenfalls zu erhalten ist.

Zurück zu den Bahnhöfen, die neben der Verkehrsfunktion ja für die Stadt auch noch weitergehende Bedeutungen haben. Woran denkt man bei diesen Projektentwicklungen in erster Linie?
Zunächst einmal daran, dass unsere Bahnhöfe dann schöner sein sollen als die von – beispielsweise – Bukarest, was derzeit nicht der Fall ist. Der Praterstern hat eine lange Bahnhofsgeschichte. Als es noch die Zeitung „Volksstimme" gab, fand man dort im Kulturteil mitunter Fotos vom Nordbahnhof mit der Information, dass da wieder einmal ein Film mit dieser Kulisse gedreht werde, um so die schlechten Zustände in Osteuropa zu zeigen. Das hatte noch Berechtigung, solange die alte Ruine des Nordbahnhofs dort stand. Dann war es eine Zeitlang in Ordnung, aber in den vergangenen zehn Jahren hätte man das auch am neueren Bahnhof Wien Nord drehen können.

Is that a completely new line?
Yes. It is not long, only about 13 km but once we have it means that intercity trains from Budapest and Bratislava, from Linz and St. Pölten can travel directly to the airport. This will increase the airport's catchment area enormously. This is the situation regarding long-distance transport. As regards local transport there is an offer made by the municipality of Vienna and the Mayor that the City Air Train (CAT) could be extended to Bratislava and thus connect to the airport there. This is somewhat difficult because there is no rail line that runs directly past the airport.
This means that a new rail line must be built there also. How far advanced are discussions with Slovakia on this rail extension to Bratislava? And does the Slovak side also plan to make an investment?
As far as I am aware they don't yet have such plans, but we will be able to provide a facility that will not involve any major disadvantages for the users. We can extend the CAT along the tracks of the old Pressburg railway line as far as Wolfsthal and from there it should be easy to set up a bus connection to Bratislava airport.

But that would mean passengers would have to change from the train to the bus.
True, but the old train cutting still exists and the line can be reconstructed. The ground is owned by the community of Wolfsthal and can be reacquired by the Federal Railways. But there is another interesting project between Vienna and Bratislava that I am particularly keen on because it represents an innovation for both cities: that is the possibility to travel from city centre to city centre by boat. At present the situation is that to travel to Budapest by boat you have to go to Handelskai and you leave from the Reichsbrücke. The area around there, Mexicoplatz, does not exactly have a great reputation and is not particularly attractive.

And therefore the boats will leave from Schwedenplatz?
Exactly, this is the entire point. The boats will leave from Schwedenplatz and thus offer an opportunity to travel downstream from the centre of Vienna to the centre of Bratislava in less than an hour. The return journey will take a little longer, but the boat trip to Bratislava would be somewhat shorter than the same journey by train.

Do the relevant studies exist?
Studies are being made. The question is whether to set up a service on demand or a regular scheduled service, i.e. one or two boats with connections in the morning and afternoon. I think it is sensational that we can connect Vienna and Bratislava by boat and can also show that there is something very interesting between these two cities – the green heart of the region, the national park, which is certainly to be preserved.

But let's go back to the railway stations, which, in addition to their transport function, have another importance for the city. What are the primary considerations in developing projects of this kind?
First of all one major consideration is that our stations should be more attractive than the ones in, for example, Bucharest, which isn't the case at the moment. Praterstern has a long railway history. When the newspaper "Volksstimme" was still being published the culture section in one issue showed photographs of Nordbahnhof (North Railway Station) with the information that yet another film was being made there using the station as a backdrop to depict the poor conditions in Eastern Europe. This was, in a way, understandable – as

Neue Bahnhöfe

Glücklicherweise wird Wien Nord jetzt umgebaut. Das Projekt von Albert Wimmer ist hervorragend, es ist, glaube ich, auch deshalb eine deutliche Verbesserung, weil es auch einen neuen Zugang zur Entwicklung des Nordbahnhofareals bietet. Da haben wir sicher gemeinsam mit der Bahn deutlich bessere Möglichkeiten, man erreicht dann auch leichter die U-Bahnlinie U1. Podreccas Platzgestaltungsprojekt wird uns den Bereich zwischen der Bahntrasse und der Praterstraße in einem völlig neuen Licht sehen lassen, allerdings erst, wenn die neue Verlängerung der U-Bahnlinie U2 fertig gestellt ist, also erst nach 2008. Zum Westbahnhof habe ich mittlerweile die Information der Bundesbahnen, dass er sehr rasch nach den Plänen von Neumann und Steiner umgebaut werden soll, zumindest, was die Halle betrifft und das Zusatzgebäude Richtung Mariahilfer Straße. Damit ist der Anfang gemacht, jedoch leider noch nicht die Symmetrie mit dem zweiten Bau Richtung Felberstraße hergestellt, aber immerhin. Damit rückt der Westbahnhof dann auch deutlich näher zur Mariahilfer Straße, da auch die unterirdische Passage dorthin verlängert wird...

Gibt es schon einen konkreten Bautermin für das Neumann/Steiner-Projekt?

Da müssten Sie bei den Bundesbahnen nachfragen. Ich glaube aber, dass im Zusammenhang mit dem neuen Zentralbahnhof auch die Baugeschwindigkeit für den Westbahnhof erhöht wird. Die Idee ist, dass man jetzt am Südbahnhof und am Ostbahnhof den Betrieb einstellt und in der Zwischenzeit den Westbahnhof nutzt, damit man schneller den Bahnhof Wien Europa Mitte bauen kann. Und da muss man vorher mit dem Westbahnhof fertig sein. Das würde bedeuten, dass wir in den nächsten zwei Jahren eine Großbaustelle am Westbahnhof haben. Ich hoffe, es ist wahr, als Wiener Stadtrat kann ich es mir nur wünschen. Finanzieren und bauen muss es die Bundesbahn. Jedenfalls hätten wir dann innerhalb eines Jahrzehnts alle drei wichtigen Bahnhöfe Wiens neu gestaltet und renoviert.

Das wichtigste Projekt ist natürlich der „Zentralbahnhof" und das Stadtentwicklungsgebiet dahinter. Was erwarten Sie dafür?

Ich wurde des Öfteren von Feuilletonisten für den Namen „Bahnhof Wien Europa Mitte" kritisiert. Dieser Name ist zwischen Stadt und Bundesbahnen gewachsen, und ich sage auch warum: Es war mir sehr wichtig, die Philosophie zu vermitteln, dass Wien ein Knotenpunkt in Mitteleuropa ist, und dass dieses Projekt der Bahnhof ist, der das repräsentiert und darstellt. Wenn Sie zurückdenken: Vor drei Jahren gab es bei den Bundesbahnen durchaus maßgebliche Herren, die der Meinung waren, dass wir das nicht brauchen, der Bahnhof Meidling könne diese Funktion auch erfüllen. Ernsthaft! Wenn der Lainzer Tunnel fertig ist, dann fährt jeder Zug auch durch den bestehenden Bahnhof Meidling zum Südbahnhof. Und dann könne man die Fernzüge durch den Steudeltunnel unter dem Südbahnhof durchziehen und Richtung Ostbahn fahren lassen. Technisch möglich – aber kein Symbol! Eine Stadt, sie sich international präsentieren möchte, braucht einen Bahnhof als Symbol, der alle Stücke spielt. Diese Idee war nicht zu promoten mit „Zentralbahnhof", das ist ein technischer Begriff. Daher: „Wien Europa Mitte". Und das hat insofern gewirkt, als dann auch Banken und andere Einrichtungen, die Headquarters für Mitteleuropa suchen, sich ernsthaft mit diesem Standort beschäftigt haben.

Können Sie da Namen nennen?

So, wie es derzeit aussieht, werden die Österreichischen Bundesbahnen mit einer sehr großen, sehr einflussreichen österreichischen Bank, die in Mittel- und Osteuropa sehr aktiv ist,

long as the ruins of the old bombed Nordbahnhof were still standing. And when this station was replaced conditions there were more or less OK for a while, but during the last ten years it would have been perfectly possible to make a similar kind of film again at Wien Nord, the station that replaced the old bombed building.

New Railway Stations

Thankfully, this station is being completely redesigned. Albert Wimmer's project is excellent. I believe it is also a clear improvement because it offers a new approach to the development of the Nordbahnhof site. We certainly have better chances if we can collaborate with the railway authorities and it will be also be easier to reach the U1 Underground line. Podrecca's redesign of the outdoor space will enable us to see the area between the train tracks and Praterstrasse in a completely new light, but only, it must be said, when the new extension of the U2 has been completed, i.e. after 2008. As regards Westbahnhof (Western Railway Station) the Austrian Federal Railways have informed me that they intended to start building to the designs by Neumann and Steiner as soon as possible – as far as the concourse and the additional building near Mariahilfer Strasse are concerned. This is a start but will not provide the symmetry that the planned second building on Felberstrasse would offer, but all the same. The Westbahnhof will be far better linked with Mariahilfer Strasse, as the underground passageway will be extended in that direction.

Is there a concrete construction schedule for the Neumann/Steiner project?

This you must ask the Austrian Federal Railways. I believe that in conjunction with the new central railway station the pace of construction at Westbahnhof will also be stepped up. The idea is that operations at the old Südbahnhof and Ostbahnhof (South and East Railway Stations) will be closed down and Westbahnhof will be used as a substitute in the intervening period to allow the new central railway station, Wien- Europa Mitte (near the old Südbahnhof), to be erected as quickly as possible. This means that the Westbahnhof redevelopment must be finished first. This in turn would mean that for the next two years Westbahnhof would be a major building site. I hope I am making it clear that, as Viennese Town Councillor this can only be a wish on my part, as financing and construction are a matter for the Federal Railways. But if all goes according to plan this would mean that we would have redesigned and renovated all three important railway stations in Vienna within the space of a decade.

The most important project is, of course, the Central Railway Station and the urban development area behind it. What are your expectations for this area?

I have been often criticised by journalists for the name of the station "Bahnhof Wien – Europa Mitte" (Vienna – Europe Central). This name was coined by the municipal authorities with the Federal Railways and I can tell you why: it was regarded as most important to convey the philosophy that Vienna is a node point in central Europe and that this railway station presents and represents this fact. If you look back: only three years ago there were important managers in the railway authorities who were of the opinion that we did not need this new station as the existing station at Meidling could fulfil this function. Seriously! The argument was that on completion of the Lainz tunnel all trains could travel through the station at Meidling to the Südbahnhof. And long- distance trains could travel through the Steudeltunnel under Südbahnhof and connect with the Ostbahn. Technically

Boris Podrecca, B. Edelmülller, W. Sobek
Praterstern, Bahnhof Wien Nord, Ansicht von der Stadt | Vienna North Station Plaza, view from the city

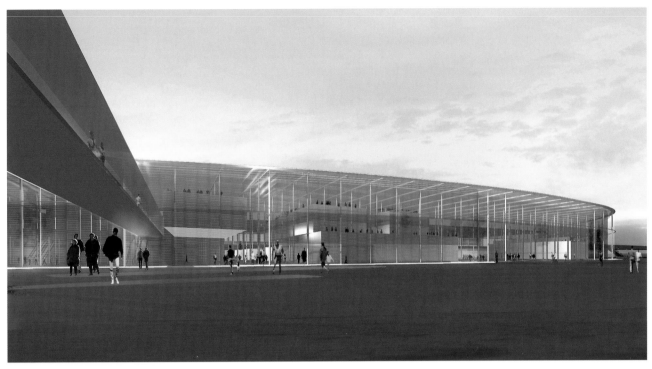

Boris Podrecca, B. Edelmülller, W. Sobek
Praterstern, Bahnhof Wien Nord, Ansicht vom Prater | Vienna North Station Plaza, view from Prater

dort deren Headquarter errichten. Wie der Bahnhof dann im künftigen Fahrplan heißen wird, ist ein anderes Thema. Der aktuelle Name hat seinen Zweck erfüllt und wir haben damit promotet: Wien braucht einen Knotenpunkt für Mitteleuropa. Und damit interessiert man auch Wirtschaftsunternehmen, die in Mitteleuropa aktiv sind. Das ist gelungen. Der zweite Schritt, der jetzt in Richtung altem Frachtenbahnhof gedacht werden muss, ist mit dem Masterplan gesetzt. Ich glaube, dass die Kombination von Albert Wimmer mit Hotz und Hoffmann und die intensive Mitarbeit unserer Abteilungen ein sehr gutes Ergebnis erbracht hat, das auch umsetzbar ist. Wir haben zum Beispiel die Chance, das Wohngebiet entlang der Sonnwendgasse gegenüber der Feuerwehr bis hinauf zur Gudrunstraße sehr rasch zu ergänzen. Die Menschen, die dort hinziehen, werden von Beginn an eine sehr gute Versorgungsqualität haben.

Dieser Teil des alten Frachtenbahnhofs bzw. des neuen Stadtentwicklungsgebiets kann noch vor dem Bahnhof in Angriff genommen werden?
Das kann, sobald die Ausmietungen erfolgt sind, in Angriff genommen werden. Wir haben dort zur U-Bahnstation Keplerplatz eine Distanz von nur 400 bis 500 Metern – das ist Gehdistanz. Und wir haben mit der Favoritenstraße eine Einkaufsstraße, die sich zwar durchaus noch erneuern kann, die aber Qualität bietet. Wir haben auch den Viktor-Adler-Markt, wir haben Schulen in diesem Bereich, man kann also sofort einziehen und Favoriten verstärken.

Das neue Favoriten
Wenn es dann in die nächsten Entwicklungsbereiche weitergeht, dann sind natürlich eine eigene Schule und eine eigene Parkanlage notwendig und dann wird es auch sinnvoll sein, dass wir die Straßenbahnlinie D durch das Gebiet führen, damit innerhalb des Gebiets auch eine hohe Qualität des öffentlichen Verkehrs geboten werden kann. Entlang der Eisenbahngleise Richtung Osten werden wir ausreichend Platz für Gewerbebetriebe haben, die noch lärmintensiv sind, für neue Büros, die mit ordentlichem Schallschutz durchaus eine Bahnanlage vertragen. Dort brauchen wir nicht mit Wohnungen hinzugehen. Ich denke, dass das eine sehr nette Mischung von Wohnen und Arbeiten werden kann, wiewohl ich weiß, dass nicht jeder, der in diesem Viertel wohnt, auch in diesem Viertel arbeiten wird.

In Wien gibt es auch „Investorenstädtebau": Stichworte Monte Laa und Wienerberg. Sind in Zukunft ähnliche Projekte zu erwarten und wie sieht die Stadtentwicklungsperspektive für diese beiden Gebiete aus?
Ich hätte unter „Investorenstädtebau" auch etwas anderes verstanden, zum Beispiel die „Dresdner Spange" und ähnliches, wo man feststellen muss, dass es gut gelungen ist, ein altes Industrieareal entlang der Bahn umzugestalten. Freilich könnte die Architektur spektakulärer sein, aber von der Funktionalität her und dem Umbau der Stadt hat das dort sehr gut funktioniert. Die beiden von Ihnen genannten Bereiche Monte Laa und Wienerberg sind Sonderfälle. Wenn Sie beispielsweise den Twin Tower von Massimiliano Fuksas nehmen, dann ist das hervorragende und spannende Architektur, ein Landmark, das weit ins Wiener Becken hineinwirkt. Wir haben daneben den Wohnbau, der sehr dicht geworden ist und davon leben wird, dass vorgelagert im Süden große Freiflächen zur Verfügung stehen. Nur damit wird sich für die Bewohner auch genügend Erholungs- und Freiraum bieten, der auf dem Gebiet selbst nicht zur Verfügung steht.

this would have been feasible – but it would not have been a symbol! A city that wants to present itself internationally needs a railway station as a symbol that can play a number of different roles. The idea was to avoid using the term Central Railway Station in the promotion work, as it is far too technical a term, hence the name Wien Europa Mitte. It has worked in the sense that banks and other businesses and facilities that are a looking for central European headquarters are seriously considering this location.

Can you name any names?
It seems at present as if the Austrian Federal Railways, together with a very large and very influential Austrian bank that is extremely active in central and eastern Europe, will erect the latter's headquarters there. The name of the station used in railway timetables etc. is a completely different matter. This name (Wien Europa Mitte) has served its purpose and we have used it in our promotions. Vienna needs a node for central Europe. And with a node of this kind one can stimulate the interest of companies that are active in central Europe. We have succeeded in doing this. The second step, which involves the old freight station, follows the master plan. I believe that the combination of Albert Wimmer with Hotz and Hoffmann and the intensive collaboration with our municipal departments has achieved excellent results that can also be practically implemented. For example, we have the chance to rapidly extend the residential area along Sonnwendgasse opposite the fire station as far as Gudrunstrasse. The people who move there will have an excellent infrastructure of facilities and amenities from the very start.

Can work on this part of the old freight station and on the new urban development area be started before the construction of the new central railway station begins?
It can be started once the existing rental agreements have been terminated. The distance to the Underground station at Keplerplatz is only 400 to 500 metres – this is walking distance. And Favoritenstrasse is a shopping street that, although it could doubtless do with renewal, offers a certain level of quality. We also have the Viktor Adler Market and there are schools in this district, which means that people can move in immediately and begin to strengthen Favoriten as a district.

The new Favoriten District
If these areas continue to develop, then naturally we will need a local school and car parking facilities, and it would make sense to continue the D tram through the district so that we can offer a high standard of public transport within the district also. Along the railway line, towards the east, we will have adequate space for businesses that produce a lot of noise, for new offices that, if provided with adequate acoustic insulation, can certainly tolerate the proximity of the railway. We don't need to build apartments there. I think that this could be a very nice mix of housing and workplace although, of course, I know that not everyone that lives in this district will work there.

In Vienna there is also the phenomenon of "urban planning by investors", the buzzwords here are Monte Laa and Wienerberg. Should we expect further similar projects in the future and what is the urban development perspective for these two districts?
I would have envisaged something else under the term "investors urban planning", for example the "Dresdner Spange" (a different redevelopment area in Vienna) or similar, where one can safely assert that the conversion of an old

Massimiliano Fuksas
Twin Towers (Detail), Wienerberg City
PHOTO ANNA BLAU

Cuno Brullmann
Wohnbau | apartment block Wienerberg City

Hätte die Stadt es nicht auf dem Genehmigungsweg in der Hand gehabt, dem entgegenzusteuern?
Sie haben vollkommen Recht. Man hat sich damals, glaube ich, vom großen Namen Fuksas beim Masterplan blenden lassen. Die Lösungen für Probleme, die damit in Verbindung stehen, liegen wie gesagt im bereits vorhandenen öffentlichen Freiraum. Ich glaube, dass sich der gesamte öffentliche Bereich am Wienerberg mit den Seen und dem Naturschutzgebiet für die BewohnerInnen sehr gut nutzen lässt. Die schulische Infrastruktur und Kindergärten werden nachgerüstet oder demnächst fertig gestellt. Der Bereich öffentlicher Verkehr ist nicht ganz so einfach. Meine erste Überlegung war es, dort eine Straßenbahnlinie entlang der Wienerbergstraße hinzubekommen, was aber daran scheiterte, dass im Untergrund dieser Straße alle wichtigen Versorgungsleitungen für Erdgas, Fernwärme, Wasser, Kanal usw. liegen. Darauf eine Straßenbahnlinie zu legen, hätte sehr hohe Erhaltungskosten bedeutet. Wir haben uns daher entschlossen, bei einer Bustrasse zu bleiben und haben eine Lösung gefunden, die gar nicht auffällt, aber dennoch den Busverkehr deutlich beschleunigt. Wir haben die modernste Signaltechnologie eingesetzt, mit welcher der Bus die Möglichkeit hat, sowohl die Ampeln auf Grün zu schalten als auch die Grünphase für sich zu erhalten. Das funktioniert blendend, fällt den anderen Verkehrsteilnehmern nicht auf und der Bus ist trotzdem schneller. Langfristig denken wir, wenn wir weiterhin die Finanzierung für die U-Bahn sicherstellen können – was zur Zeit nicht der Fall ist, weil der Bundesanteil für die nächste Ausbauphase noch fehlt

industrial area along a railway line has really been successful. Naturally, the architecture there could be more spectacular, but in terms of function and the conversion of the city it performs extremely well. The two examples you mention, Monte Laa and Wienerberg, are special cases. The Twin Tower by Massimiliano Fuksas is an excellent and exciting piece of architecture, a landmark that exerts its visual effect far into the Vienna Basin. But on the other hand the housing has grown very dense and will live from the fact that there are large areas of outdoor space in front of it to the south. Only in this way is it possible to offer residents enough space for recreation and leisure activities, in the immediate district this space is simply not available.

Did the planning permission process not offer the City of Vienna an effective instrument to counter this development?
You are entirely right. I think at the time people allowed themselves be dazzled by the big names in the master plan, such as Fuksas. As has been said already the solution to the problems here lies in the existing areas of public space. I believe that the entire public outdoor area on Wienerberg with the lakes and the nature reserve offers an amenity that can be utilized by the residents. The infrastructure of schools and kindergartens is being improved and will shortly be completed. The matter of public transport is not so simple. My first idea was to run a tramline along Wienerbergstrasse but this plan was thwarted by the fact that all the important pipes

Wienerberg City: Gesamtansicht von Osten | General view from east
PHOTO ANNA BLAU

– in der fünften Ausbauphase etwa ab 2020 daran, die U-Bahn-linie 2, die künftig auf dem Areal hinter dem Bahnhof Wien-Europa-Mitte enden soll, über den Reumannplatz zum Wiener-berg zu verlängern. Dann hätten wir den gesamten westlichen Teil Favoritens ebenfalls an die U-Bahn angebunden und einen schönen Endpunkt mit entsprechend großem Bevölkerungspo-tenzial, das an der U-Bahn wohnt.

Für wie realistisch halten Sie, dass der Bundesanteil hier zumindest in Sichtweite kommt?
Wir sind mit dem Verkehrsministerium handelseins, allein der Finanzminister ist offensichtlich zu sehr mit anderen Angele-genheiten beschäftigt, um sich mit der Wiener U-Bahn zu be-fassen. Wir wissen auf Beamtenebene, dass der Finanzierungs-schlüssel weiterhin vom Bund akzeptiert wird, es geht nur um die Höhe. Hier betreibt der Finanzminister offenbar Parteipolitik gegen Wien durchaus mit Billigung des Herrn Bundeskanzlers.

Zum Stichwort Monte Laa gibt es ja ganz ähnliche Probleme, unser Begriff „Investorenstädtebau" ist durchaus polemisch gemeint. Im Gebiet Monte Laa hat die Porr Großes bewirkt, wie war deren Einfluss auf die Stadtplanungsprozeduren?
Sie befragen mich über eine Zeit, in der ich noch nicht Stadt-rat war. Die Weichen dafür sind lang vor meiner Zeit gestellt worden. Ich möchte mich aber nicht daraus verabschieden und glaube, dass wir mit dem Abschluss bei der Absberggas-se, mit dem Porrgebäude als Gelenk zur Laaer-Berg-Straße hin,

for gas, heating, drainage etc. lie beneath this street. To build a tram line on top of this would have meant extremely high maintenance costs. We therefore decided to stick with the solution of a bus line and have found a solution that, while it is perhaps not immediately striking nevertheless clearly accelerates bus traffic. We have used the most modern traffic light technology that allows the bus driver both to change the lights to green or to keep them green when the bus is approaching a junction. This functions extremely well, the motorists don't really notice it and the bus moves faster. In the long term we think that, if we can secure the financing of the Underground – which at the moment is far from certain, as the federal government contribution for the next develop-ment phase has not yet been paid – in the fifth phase, that is from about 2020, we will further extend the U2 (the extension presently under construction is planned to end on the site behind the new central railway station) across Reumannplatz to Wienerberg. This would mean that the entire western part of Favoriten would also be connected to the Underground system and we would have an excellent terminal on the line, with a suitably large sector of the population living close to the Underground.

How likely do you think it is that the State will pay at least part of its share?
We have reached agreement with the transport ministry but the minister of finance is apparently too occupied with other

Coop Himmelb(l)au
Wienerberg City: Sky loops

PHOTOS ANNA BLAU

Delugan-Meissl
Wienerberg City: apartment tower (Hintergrund | background)

Hans Hollein, Albert Wimmer
Monte Laa mit | with towers
PHOTO PORR AG

und der Verbindung zur Wohnbebauung, die beim Laaer Wald schon entstanden war, durchaus vertreten können, dass dort noch weitere Verdichtung stattfindet.

Sie meinen die Wohnbebauung der Stadt Wien?
Ja, und natürlich ist diese Verdichtung ungewöhnlich, wir hätten natürlich genügend gewachsenen Grund. Aber wenn jemand das Risiko auf sich nimmt, über Autobahnen zu bauen, dann wird er schon wissen warum.

Stadtentwicklungsgebiete im Süden und Hochhäuser
Wir wollen, wenn die U-Bahnlinie 1 nach Süden Richtung Rothneusiedl verlängert ist, dann die dort nicht mehr benötigte Straßenbahnlinie 67 aus der Favoritenstraße herauskippen und zum Monte Laa führen. Damit wäre auch die Frage beantwortet, ob der Bus ausreicht oder nicht und das wird in ein paar Jahren so weit sein.

Gibt es genügend Entwicklungsdruck für die geplante Verlängerung der U-Bahnlinie 1 bis Rothneusiedl? Es wurde ja für dieses Gebiet ein Stadionneubau diskutiert, eine Lobby drängt, dass sich dort der Fußballclub Austria entsprechend präsentieren kann. Wird die Stadt diesem Austria-Begehren eine beschleunigte Planung von Rothneusiedl folgen lassen?
Der springende Punkt ist, ob die Grundeigentümer dort ein Stadion wollen. Ich sehe zurzeit noch nicht, dass die Austria oder deren Präsident oder andere mit der Austria eng Verbundene die Eigentümerstrukturen in dieser Gegend verändert hätten. Im Gegenteil habe ich aber den Eindruck, dass die aktuellen Eigentümer der Liegenschaften große Euro-Zeichen in den Augen haben, wenn sie von der Austria sprechen. Allerdings glaube ich nicht, dass Frank Stronach die Grundeigentümer dort genauso fördern will, wie er Gönner der Austria ist. Ohne

matters to bother with the Vienna Underground system. At civil service level we know that the federal government has accepted the structure of the financing, the issue is the amount – and here the minister is clearly waging a party political campaign against Vienna with the complete approval of the Federal Chancellor.

There are similar problems regarding Monte Laa, our term "investors urban planning" is meant polemically. In the area of Monte Laa the Porr Company has had an enormous effect, what was the influence on the urban planning procedure?
You are asking me about a time before I was city councillor. The plans had been determined long before my time. I don't want to avoid the issue however and I believe that to terminate with Absberggasse, using the Porr Building as a joint to Laaer Berg Strasse and connecting to the housing development already existing at Laaer Wald we could reasonably propose a further increase in density there.

You mean the municipal housing development?
Yes, and of course this level of density is unusual, as there is enough building land available nearby, but if someone decides to take the risk of building across the motorway then surely he must be aware of what he is doing.

Urban Development Areas in the South of the City and High-Rise Buildings
Once the U1 Underground line has been extended south to Rothneusied we want to divert the 67 tramline (that won't be needed any longer there) from Favoritenstrasse and to run it towards Monte Laa.

Does the level of development pressure justify plans to extend the U1 Underground Line to Rothneusiedl? A new stadium

Monte Laa in Bau | under construction, 2005

Monte Laa: Luftansicht im Endausbau | Future air view

Peter Podsedensek
„Komet" development mit | with tower

Stadtentwicklungsgebiet Kabelwerk
Urban development Kabelwerk, Wien-Meidling

Grundstückstransaktionen zu vernünftigen Preisen wird es dieses Projekt wohl nicht geben.

Damit fällt dann auch die Verlängerung der U-Bahnlinie 1?
Damit würde die U-Bahnlinie 1 sehr wohl verlängert, allerdings nur bis zur Per-Albin-Hansson-Siedlung. Solange es nicht gelingt, im Bereich Rothneusiedl Wohnen, Arbeiten und Unterhaltung wie etwa ein Stadion unterzubringen, solange macht es keinen Sinn, zu verlängern.

Damit hängt auch das Thema Hochhäuser und Hochhaus-Konzept zusammen. Es gibt hier aktuell ein breites Spektrum an Planungen von der Innenstadt bis zu weiter außerhalb gelegenen Gebieten. Können Sie vielleicht kurz den Stand der Dinge aus Sicht der Stadt darstellen?
Kurz zum Rahmen: In der Nachkriegszeit galt die Doktrin: „Keine Hochhäuser in dieser Stadt!" Sie ist aber bald durchbrochen worden, etwa bei der UNO-City. Ich habe es auch schon damals für falsch gehalten, so eine apodiktische Ablehnung von Hochhäusern zu statuieren. Planungsstadtrat Hannes Swoboda hat das dann in seiner Zeit glücklicherweise aufgehoben. Es gab immer wieder Versuche von Architekturgruppen

building has been proposed for this area, and a lobby urges that the Austria soccer club should be allowed present itself there in a suitable setting. Will the City of Vienna accelerate the planning of Rothneusiedl in response to the wishes of the Austria club?
The important point is whether the property owners there want a stadium. I see no signs at present that *Austria* or its president or any other close associate of the club has undertaken anything to alter the ownership structure in this area. On the contrary, I have the impression that the current owners of the sites see large euro signs in front of their eyes whenever they speak about the *Austria* club. However, I don't believe that *Austria* president Frank Stronach wants to enrich the property owners there just because he is a generous patron of the club. Without property transactions at reasonable prices this project is unlikely to happen.

Does this mean that the U1 Underground line will not be extended?
This means that the U1 could indeed be extended but only as far as the Per-Albin-Hansson housing estate. Until it is possible to combine housing, work and entertainment (such as

und Städteplanern, ein Hochhauskonzept für Wien zustande zu bringen. Das ist meinen Vorgängern leider nicht gelungen und glücklicherweise konnten wir uns nun darauf einigen. Ich glaube, dass das jetzige Konzept sehr gut funktioniert. Wir haben nicht a priori Zonen von Hochhäusern festgelegt. Die Grundeigentümer hätten sofort zu spekulieren begonnen. Wir haben daher definiert, dass man dorthin geht, wo der öffentliche Verkehr und die Anbindungsqualität hervorragend sind, und erst später entscheidet, ob ein Hochhaus hinkommen soll oder nicht, weil ja viele andere Faktoren auch noch mitspielen. Wir wollen Hochhäuser nicht dort, wo der öffentliche Verkehr schlecht ist. Sie werden vielleicht einwenden, dass es dazu einige Beispiele gäbe. Dort haben wir versucht, den öffentlichen Verkehr zu verbessern, wie vorhin dargestellt. Wir haben auch gesagt, dass es einige Zonen gibt, wo Hochhäuser aus Sicht der Stadt sinnvoll sind. Zum Beispiel ist es sinnvoll, in der Donau-City weiter zu bauen. Es ist aus Sicht der Stadt auch sinnvoll, die Dominanz eines Bereichs zu unterstützen, nämlich das Donaukanalufer im zweiten Bezirk, und gleich anschließend bei der Uniqa den Wienfluss hinauf.

Wien-Mitte, Zentralbahnhof und Schönbrunn – wird es auch hier neue Wolkenkratzer geben?
Die Verdichtung bei Wien-Mitte ist kein architektonisches oder städtebauliches Problem, sondern ein ökonomisches. Das alte Projekt ist mit Sicherheit nicht am Weltkulturerbe allein gescheitert. Das neue Projekt ist deutlich besser und ich bin froh, dass ich diesen Wettbewerb damals angesagt habe, obwohl es verwegen war, bei einer aufrechten Baubewilligung noch einen städtebaulichen Wettbewerb zu starten. Wir haben auch am Südbahnhof kein Problem, dass dort Hochhäuser entstehen, soferne sie nicht den Blick vom Unteren zum Oberen Belvedere beleidigen, also sozusagen den umgekehrten Canaletto-Blick. Wir hätten auch am Westbahnhof damit kein Problem gehabt, das Projekt Neumann-Steiner kommt ohne Hochhäuser aus, was zeigt, dass es sowohl von der Architektur als auch von der wirtschaftlichen Verwertbarkeit her nicht unbedingt notwendig ist, hoch zu bauen. Es hätte dort aber, glaube ich auch, ein Akzent gepasst. Und wir haben privaten Investoren offen gelassen, dass sie selbst Standorte entwickeln und uns beweisen, dass der Standort funktionieren kann, denn einen zweiten Florido-Tower wollte ich nicht unbedingt haben. So ist jetzt auch von den Investoren beim „Komet" dieses Verfahren begonnen worden, sie haben den städtebaulichen Wettbewerb abgewickelt und – wie nicht anders zu erwarten war – ist im Nahbereich von Schönbrunn eine vergleichbare Diskussion entstanden wie bei Wien-Mitte, die ebenfalls mit nicht ganz richtigen Darstellungen von den Perspektiven und Sichtachsen gewürzt wurde. Im Nahbereich der „Komet" Gründe gibt es bereits ein höheres Gebäude, das Meidlinger Hochhaus mit seiner merkwürdigen Form und Fassadengestaltung. Dort etwas dazuzusetzen, das vielleicht architektonisch bessere Qualität hat, dagegen spräche aus meiner Sicht nichts. Die Frage ist, wie dicht und wie hoch das werden muss. Ich habe nichts dagegen, dort im Rahmen der immer schon möglichen Kubatur etwas Schöneres hinzubringen als Fabrikshallen. Ich denke, das wird auch gelingen.

Zusammenfassend kann man sagen, dass das Hochhaus-Konzept eher auf Armlänge praktiziert wird, als dass ein Dogma ausgegeben wird wie „kein Hochhaus" oder „Hochhäuser nur an politisch festgelegten Standorten".
Wien ist in einer anderen Situation als Innsbruck. Innsbruck hat sich etwa zur selben Zeit sehr intensiv mit Hochhäusern beschäftigt und ist zu einem logischen Schluss gekommen: Wenn Hochhäuser, dann kann man sie nur am Südrand der Stadt bau-

a stadium, for instance) in the Rothneusiedl area it makes no sense to extend the U1 there.

The theme of high-rise buildings and high-rise concepts is also related to this issue. At the moment there is a wide spectrum of plans for such buildings, ranging from the inner city to districts far outside the centre. Can you explain the state of things to us from the viewpoint of the municipal administration?
Firstly, as regards the framework: in the post-war period the doctrine was: "no high-rise buildings in this city". But this doctrine was soon modified, for instance in the case of the UNO City. Even at that time I thought it wrong to formulate this kind of apodictic rejection of high-rise buildings. Happily the town councillor for planning at the time, Hannes Swoboda, revoked this prohibition during his term of office. Groups of architects and urban planners made repeated attempts to develop a high-rise concept for Vienna. Unfortunately my predecessors did not succeed but happily we have recently been able to agree on such a concept. I believe that this concept works extremely well. We do not lay down zones for high-rise buildings a priori. If we did the site owners would immediately start to speculate. We have therefore said: the principle is that development should take place where public transport and existing connections are excellent and that the decision on whether a high-rise should be built at a specific location or not will only be made later, as there are many other functions involved. We do not want to have high-rise buildings where public transport is poor. Perhaps you will object that there are already number of high-rise buildings where this is the case. In such cases we have attempted to improve public transport, as I outlined above. We have also said that there are a number of zones where, from the viewpoint of the city administration, high-rise buildings make sense. For example it makes sense to continue developing the Donau City. From the viewpoint of the municipal authorities it is also sensible to support the dominance of an area, namely the bank of the Danube Canal in the second district and, directly adjoining it, the area near the Uniqa building and further up the River Wien.

Wien Mitte, Central Railway Station and Schönbrunn – will there be new Skyscrapers?
The increase in density at Wien Mitte (inner city interchange station) is not an architectural or urban planning problem but an economic one. The old project was certainly not dropped just because of the threat it posed to Vienna's status as part of the UNESCO world cultural heritage. The new project is clearly better and I am happy that I set up this competition at the time despite the risks involved in starting an urban design competition while the planning permission granted to an earlier project was still valid. At Südbahnhof we won't have a problem with any high-rise buildings that might be erected there as long as they do not impair the view from the Lower Belvedere to the Upper Belvedere, that is to say looking in the opposite direction to the famous Canaletto painting. This issue would not be problem at Westbahnhof either but it does not arise there as the Neumann Steiner project dispenses with high-rise buildings.
This shows that it is not always entirely necessary to build high-rises, either from an architectural or an economic viewpoint. Yet in this particular case I think placing a certain accent would have been appropriate. And we have left it up to private investors to develop locations themselves and then to prove to us that the location can function, as I don't particularly wish to have a second Florido Tower in Vienna. The investors in the "Komet" project, for example, have already

en. Damit kommt man der inneralpinen Lage deutlich entgegen und verhindert, dass höhere Gebäude dort entstehen, wo sie auf jeden Fall im Weg wären. Die Einflugschneisen und alles, was es in Innsbruck zu beachten gilt, erlauben gar nichts anderes, als an der Südzone der Stadt höhere Häuser zu positionieren.

Subzentren, Biocluster und Universitäten

In Wien ist das glücklicherweise anders, wir sind von der Topographie nicht so eingeengt. Wir haben in den letzten 15 Jahren eine Entwicklung genommen, die mehrere Zentren neben dem dominierenden Zentrum Innenstadt zulässt. Die Innenstadt wird weiterhin dominieren, aber wir haben mit Favoriten, mit Kagran oder mit Floridsdorf auch durch die Bevölkerungsentwicklung sehr dominierende weitere Zentren. Wenn man dem durch höhere Gebäude Rechnung trägt, spricht aus meiner Sicht nichts dagegen.

Noch eine Frage zum Bereich Wissenschaft, HiTech und Bildungsbau. Wir haben zwei BioCenters, in der Muthgasse und in Erdberg, warum gibt es zwei verschiedene und welche weitere Entwicklung wird hier stattfinden? Etwa Unis an den Stadtrand hinaus – ist das grundsätzlich ein Masterplan und wie steht es konkret um das Projekt Universität für angewandte Kunst in der Donaucity?

Wir sind froh, dass rund um das IMP im dritten Bezirk so viele Spin-Offs entstehen. Die Kombination von privater und universitärer Forschung im unmittelbaren Nahbereich bietet enorme Möglichkeiten. Diese Auslagerungen in den Spin-Offs ergaben, dass St. Marx sich vom Schlachthof- zum Biotechnologie-Bezirk entwickelt hat. Der zweite Standort ermöglicht zusätzliche Synergien. Die Universität für Bodenkultur geht ja von einer anderen Forschungsrichtung an die Dinge heran als die Biologen oder die Botaniker. Es gibt hier ein leicht versetztes Aufgabengebiet. Ich denke, dass das, was die Universität für Bodenkultur dort macht, sehr wichtig und eine gute Ergänzung zu dem ist, was das IMP im Osten Wiens begonnen hat. Ich glaube, dass es inhaltliche Unterschiede gibt und dass es auch die Konkurrenz in der Forschung fördern kann. Ich glaube doch, dass es gelingen wird, aus den BOKU-Aktivitäten die Spin-Offs zu organisieren und dass die Vorbereitung dieses neuen Technologiebereiches nicht verloren ist.

Der Bereich der Angewandten bietet neue Möglichkeiten. Wenn eine Universität, die nicht extrem groß ist, merkt, dass sie an ihrem aktuellen Standort eher Schwierigkeiten hat, viele ausgelagerte Institute, ein dringendst renovierungsbedürftiges Gebäude mit all den Problemen der Umsiedlung und Zwischenumsiedlung, und wenn die Stadt dann in einem Stadtteil, in dem es wenig kulturelle Aktivitäten gibt, die Chance hat, mit einer Kunstuniversität einen Schwerpunkt dort zu setzen, wo bisher nur Wohnungen und Büros waren, dann halte ich das für sehr spannend und sehr wichtig. Wir können dort dann auch eine kulturelle Einrichtung der Stadt dazusetzen. Das Haus der Kulturen, das schon lange in Diskussion ist, würde sehr gut dazupassen.

started this process: they have held the urban design competition and – inevitably – in the area close to Schönbrunn a discussion has started similar to the one that flared up at Wien Mitte, and also spiced with perspectives and sight lines that are not entirely correct. There is already a taller building in the area near the "*Komet*" grounds, the Meidling high-rise building with its odd form and facade design. To contrast it with a building of superior architectural quality is, in my opinion, something no one could reasonably object to. The question is how dense and how high the development should be. I have no objection if what is built within the framework of the permitted volume is more attractive than factory sheds. And I think this is what will happen.

To summarise can one say that the high-rise concept is applied at an arm's length rather than by proclaiming a dogma such as "no high-rise buildings" or "high-rise buildings only at locations decided by urban policy"?

Vienna is in a different situation to Innsbruck. Innsbruck investigated the question of high-rise buildings most exhaustively at around the same time as Vienna and came to a logical conclusion: if high-rise buildings are to be erected then only at the southern perimeter of the city. This is appropriate to the city's location within the Alps and prevents the erection of taller buildings where they would be an obstruction. The flight approach paths and everything else that has to be taken into account in Innsbruck mean there is no alternative to locating taller buildings in the southern area of the city.

Sub-Centres, Bio-Clusters and Universities

In Vienna, fortunately, the situation is different; we are not so restricted by the topography. In the last 15 years we have followed a development strategy that allows several centres to co-exist alongside the dominant centre. The inner city will continue to dominate but in Favoriten, Kagran or Floridsdorf we have (due in part to the population growth pattern) very dominant additional centres. In my view, there can be no objections if taller buildings reflect this fact.

One further question about the areas of science, high-tech and educational buildings. We have two bio-centres, one in Muthgasse, the other in Erdberg, why two different locations? What direction will the future development take? Universities on the perimeter of the city perhaps – is that part of a master plan? And, in concrete terms, what is the situation about the proposals for moving the University of Applied Arts to the Donaucity?

We are happy that so many spin-offs are developing around the IMP in the third district (Erdberg). The combination of private and university research in close proximity offers enormous possibilities. This move toward spin-offs has meant that St Marx has developed from a former abattoir district into a biotechnology district. A second location allows additional synergies. The University of Agriculture approaches research in a very different way to the biologists or the botanists. This is a different area. I think that what the University is doing there is extremely important and excellent complements what the IMP has started in eastern Vienna. I think that there are differences in terms of content and emphasis and that these can stimulate competition in the area of research. I believe that it will prove possible to organize spin-offs from the BOKU's (University of Agriculture) activities and that the preparations made for this new area of technology are not a wasted effort.

The question of the University of Applied Arts offers a new opportunity. When a university that is not extremely large

Donaukanal: Media tower von | by Hans Hollein, multifunctional UNIQA tower von | by Jean Nouvel

Oder auch die Kunsthalle?
Die Kunsthalle haben wir ja schon einmal übersiedelt. Ich würde sie dort als Mitbeteiligte sehen wollen. Ob sie dann Träger
des Hauses der Kulturen sind oder jemand anderer, das sei noch
dahingestellt, aber auf jeden Fall ist sie bei der Entwicklung mit
dabei. Ich bin überzeugt davon, dass es eine hervorragende Idee
und sehr richtig ist, mit der Universität für angewandte Kunst
dorthin zu gehen. Es gibt aber auch Tendenzen der Technischen
Universität und der Wirtschaftsuniversität, sich neue Standorte zu suchen. Beides gehört nach Wien, Tulln ist wahrscheinlich nicht der große Heuler im internationalen Wettbewerb der
Wissenschaftsstandorte. Das hat auch Seibersdorf gemerkt und
viele wichtige Bereiche nach Wien zurückverlagert. Bei der
Technischen Universität gibt es zwei Fakultäten, die besonders
unter der aktuellen Situation leiden, die Technische Chemie
und die Maschinenbaufakultät, beide haben schlechte Gebäude, sind zum überwiegenden Teil disloziert. All das zusammen
zu führen macht Sinn, wir haben verschiedene Standorte in
Wien angeboten und ich hoffe, dass die Technische Universität
sich ernsthaft für einen davon entscheiden wird. Die Universität selbst stellt Überlegungen an, als Ganzes woanders hinzugehen, das wäre die Option Flugfeld Aspern für die Technische
Universität. Da muss man schon darüber nachdenken, ob eine
so große Verlagerung für die verbleibenden Gebäude und den
Karlsplatz nicht eine sehr arge Lücke wäre. Daher ist Durch-
schauen und Durchdenken gemeinsam mit der Technischen
Universität hier notwendig. Aber die beiden notleidenden Fakultäten an einem neuen Standort neu zu gruppieren, halte ich
für sehr zweckmäßig.

becomes aware of difficulties at its present location, when
many of its institutes must be housed outside the main building, when the building is in urgent need of renovation with
all the ensuing problems of moving into temporary premises
and when the city has the chance to use this art university to
place an accent in a part of the city where there are few cultural activities, where to date there are only offices and housing – then I regard this as an exciting and important opportunity. We could then add an urban cultural amenity; the Haus
der Kulturen (House of Cultures), which has been discussed for
a long time, would be a very suitable addition.

Or perhaps the Kunsthalle?
We have moved the Kunsthalle once already. I would like to
see it involved there. Whether it or someone else should run
the Haus der Kulturen is still an open matter but the Kunsthalle will certainly be involved in the development. I am
convinced that it is an excellent idea and absolutely correct to
move the University of Applied Arts there. There are also indications that the University of Technology and the University
of Economics are thinking about new locations. Both belong
in Vienna. I don't think that Tulln (which has offered itself as
a possible location) is exactly the last word when it comes to
international locations for scientific facilities. Seibersdorf has
become aware of this problem and has moved back many of
its important facilities to Vienna. In the University of Technology there are two faculties that suffer particularly under
the present situation, chemical engineering and mechanical
engineering. Both are housed in inadequate buildings and are
quite split up. Moving these two together makes sense. We
have proposed a number of different locations in Vienna and
I hope that the University of Technology can decide on one
of them. The University itself is debating whether it should
move elsewhere entirely, Aspern Airfield is one option. Here

Obwohl Berlin nicht viel Geld für Schulbau hat, gibt es gerade im Ostteil der Stadt einen großen Bedarf an zusätzlichen Räumen aufgrund des Zusatzbedarfes an Ganztagsbetreuung. Dort stellt man nun mit der alten DDR-Platte Erweiterungsgebäude neben die DDR-Schulen aus den 1960er Jahren. Im Prinzip ist Österreich ja in einer ähnlichen Situation wie Deutschland, auch wenn Wien nicht in einer ähnlichen wie Berlin ist. Wie sieht da die Perspektive aus? Wird es ein Schulbauprogramm 2010 geben?

Wir hatten ein großes Schulbauprogramm in den 1990er Jahren mit sehr großen Erfolgen und der Architekturtourismus lebt ja zu einem Teil auch davon. Wir haben zwei gänzlich unterschiedliche Probleme. In den inneren Bezirken, in den Gürtel-Bereichen und Gründerzeitvierteln haben wir zuviel Schulraum zur Verfügung. Und es gibt eine extrem starke Verlagerung von Kindern, die an die Allgemeinbildenden Höheren Schulen gehen und nicht mehr an die Mittelschule, wie die Hauptschule heutzutage heißt. Die Abstimmung über die Schulformen hat hier mit den Füßen stattgefunden, die AHS ist zur Gesamtschule geworden. Das wollen nur viele konservative Bildungspolitiker nicht wahrhaben. In den Bundesländern ist das anders.

Schulen und Creative Industries

Diese Unterschiede sind da und führen dazu, dass wir Schulen, Klassen und Schulgebäude im innerstädtischen Bereich zurücknehmen können und müssen. Sinnvoller Weise, denn sonst ist der Erhaltungsaufwand zu groß, um beste Qualität bieten könnten. Anders ist es in den Erweiterungsgebieten, vor allem im 22. Bezirk. Dort fehlen sehr viele Schultypen und sehr viele Klassen, ungefähr 200 SchülerInnen müssen über die Donau pendeln, weil etwa im Herbst 2005 bereits zu wenig Angebot für die AHS-Klassen besteht. Daher ist der Bau von Schulen jenseits der Donau sinnvoll und wir müssen antizipieren, was dort in vielleicht 20 Jahren passiert. Eigentlich müssten wir sogar wieder darüber nachdenken, ob nicht Containerschulen und temporäre Schulgebäude Sinn machen. Das mag bitter für Architekten sein, die gerne auch nach ihrem Tod noch eines Gebäudes sicher sein wollen, mit dem sie identifiziert werden. Für die öffentliche Hand ist es jedoch anders kaum finanzierbar.

Es gibt doch eine Schule in der Donaustadt aus den 1970ern von Riccabona, die er zum Umbau in einen Wohnbau geplant hat, aber das ist nie passiert?

Das ist nie passiert, weil die Donaustadt ja noch so stürmisch weiter gewachsen ist und noch weiter wachsen wird. Man kann aber trotzdem alleine von der Flächenverfügbarkeit her sagen, dass wir in manchen Teilen der Donaustadt nicht mehr weiter verdichten werden. Sollte gegen den Widerstand der ÖVP die Ganztagsschule doch zur Regel werden, dann sind viele unserer innerstädtischen Schulen auch nicht wirklich dazu geeignet und es wird sehr viel an Umbaubedarf geben. Aber das große Schulbauprogramm selbst, wo wir viele neue Schulen bauen, ist nach allen Berechnungen derzeit nicht notwendig. Zum Leidwesen der Architekten, wie ich weiß.

one would really have to examine the effect of such a major move on the old buildings and whether this move would not create too large a gap on Karlsplatz. Therefore it is necessary to examine these options together with the University. But I think it is a very good idea to group together the two faculties that are in such a difficult situation at present.

Berlin has little money for school buildings but in the eastern part of the city there is a major need for additional space due to the increased requirement for all-day care of school pupils. The historic DDR modular panel concept is currently being used to build extensions to existing DDR schools from the 1960s. In principle Austria is in a very similar situation to Germany, even if Vienna is not in quite the same position as Berlin. What are the perspectives like? Will there be a school building programme 2010?

We had a major school building programme in the 1990s and architecture tourism in Vienna lives to a certain extent from these buildings. We have two very different problems here. In the inner city areas, in the Gürtel areas and 19th century districts we have too much school space. And there is a decided tendency for children to go to the AHS (Allgemeinbildende Höhere Schule/High School) and no longer to the Mittelschule (Junior High School), as the standard secondary school is called nowadays. Parents have voted on the different school types with their (or their children's) feet, the AHS has become the comprehensive school. Many conservative education politicians are unwilling to accept this fact but in the Austrian provinces the situation is different.

Schools and Creative Industries

These differences exist and lead to the fact that we can and must reduce the number of schools, classrooms and school buildings in the inner city area. The cost of maintaining them is too great and would prevent us from continuing to offer the best quality there. In the growth areas of the city things are very different, above all in the 22nd district. Many different kinds of schools and classes are lacking there and more than 200 pupils will have to commute across the Danube because in autumn 2005 there will be too few AHS classes there. Therefore it makes sense to build schools on the far side of the Danube and we must anticipate what might happen there in, say, 20 years. In fact we really have to think whether container schools and temporary school buildings might make sense. This may be bitter pill to swallow for the architects who want to be immortalised in buildings that survive them. But for the public purse any other system is almost impossible to finance.

There is a school in the Donaustadt dating from the 1970s that was designed by Riccabona in such a way that it could be converted into a residential building. But this has never happened.

This never happened, as the Donaustadt has grown at such a pace and will continue to grow in the future. But from the amount of land available alone we can say that in many parts of the Donaustadt we will not increase the density any further. If the all-day school does become the norm despite the opposition of the ÖVP (the conservative party and the major partner in the national coalition government) then many of our inner city schools are not really suited for this function and there will be a major need for adaptations. But, according to all the calculations and studies that have been made, a large school building programme involving considerable numbers of new schools is not necessary at the moment, much to the disappointment of the architects, as I am fully aware.

Gründerzeitbezirke als eigener Wirtschaftsraum – können Sie dazu noch etwas sagen?

Die Gründerzeit wird je nach persönlicher Erfahrung und beruflicher Herkunft extrem verschieden beurteilt. Im Wohnbau ist sie mit Sicherheit nicht sehr beliebt wegen der Gangküchen und Substandardwohnungen. Sie wird aber von jenen sehr geschätzt, die Wohnen und Arbeiten gerne in unmittelbarer Nähe haben. Das funktioniert wieder besser, weil die verschmutzenden und emittierenden Betriebe jetzt in den Gründerzeitbauten nicht mehr so stark vertreten sind. Es gibt sehr schöne Beispiele im 15. Bezirk, in Fünfhaus, wo die Hinterhof-Gewerbebetriebe mutiert sind zu IT- und Softwareproduzenten oder zu kleinen Kaffeehäusern und Veranstaltungsräumen. Das halte ich alles für sehr spannend und glaube auch, dass da viel herauszuholen ist, denn es gibt die Stadtnähe und die kommunale Infrastruktur ist vorhanden. Wir haben dort eine Vielfalt an Kombinationen von täglichen Aktivitäten. Worunter dieser Bereich stark leidet, ist das Image. Und dieses Image ist verbesserungsfähig, wie man bei „Soho" in Ottakring sieht. Die Mischung von Stadt, Kulturschaffenden und Gewerbetreibenden, die begonnen haben, eine sehr unattraktive Zone wieder zu beleben, war sehr erfolgreich. Wir könnten doch, anstatt immer nur zu lamentieren, dass die Einkaufsstraßen den Bach hinuntergehen, beginnen, in Einkaufsstraßen auch andere Berufe z.B. aus dem weiteren Feld der Creative Industries in der Erdgeschoßzone anzusiedeln. Es spricht doch überhaupt nichts dagegen, dass sich Architektur- und Planerbüros in der Erdgeschoßzone befinden. Was wir sehen müssen und noch 2005 durchgehen werden, ist die Frage, ob die Breitbandversorgung, die man fraglos heutzutage für solche Unternehmen braucht, in den betreffenden Straßen vorhanden ist, ob man nachrüsten kann, ob man dann die freistehenden Lokalitäten auch durch das „Wir leiten ein…"-Angebot an den Hauseigentümer mobilisieren kann und er im Gegenzug aber auch den Preis für das aufgewertete Lokal entsprechend niedrig hält. Denn die Freigabe der Mietzinse, das Abschaffen der Obergrenzen de facto, ist ja nicht nur im Wohnungsbereich von Nachteil, sondern auch bei den gewerblichen Lokalen. Hier erwarte ich mir, dass wir die eine oder andere eher schlecht gehende Geschäftsstraße mit neuem Leben ergänzen.

Mietobergrenzen können Sie von der Stadt ja nicht verordnen?

Nein, das ist ein Gentlemen's Agreement, der Eigentümer bekommt aber dafür Breitband und wir bekommen längere Zeit die Mieten herunter für die, die einziehen wollen.

Wir danken für das Gespräch.

19th century residential areas as an independent economic area, can you say something about this?

Everyone assesses the Gründerzeit (19th century) areas differently according to their personal experience and professional background. In the field of housing they are certainly not much loved on account of the kitchens that open directly onto the access hallway and one to the sub-standard apartments. But these districts are popular with those who like to have their place of work and their home close together. This now functions better because there are no longer so many noisy and dirty businesses in the Gründerzeit areas. There are a number of fine examples in the 15th district in Fünfhaus where the backyard businesses have transformed into information technology and software producers, or into small coffee shops and events spaces. I regard all of this as most exciting and also believe that a great deal can be gained from such places thanks to their proximity to the city and their communal infrastructure. There is a varied combination of different daily activities in such areas. But they do suffer seriously in terms of image. And this image can be improved, as one can see from SOHO in Ottakring. The mixture of city, culturally active persons and business people that began to revive a very unattractive zone has proved highly successful. But instead of always complaining that the shopping streets are going downhill we could start to introduce other professions, from the broad area of the creative industries for instance, into the ground floor zones. There can be no objection to locating architects and planners offices in former ground floor shops. What we must look at and will examine in 2005 is the question whether broadband Internet, which is doubtless essential for such businesses nowadays, is available in these streets, whether this service can be installed and whether empty premises can be mobilised by installing such new services for property owners on the condition that the rent for the improved property is kept low. After all, the changes made to the rent restriction laws, where there is now practically no upper limit, have created a problem not just in the area of housing but in the area of commercial premises also. Here I expect that we will be able to introduce new life to one or two of the shopping streets that at present are in a rather sad state.

But the city cannot set an upper limit to rents?

No, this would be a gentleman's agreement but the advantage for the property owner would be that broadband would be installed while we would have lower rents for a longer period for those who want to move into the premises.

Thank you for giving us this interview.

Das Gespräch fand am 25. April 2005 statt.

The interview took place on April 25, 2005

STEP 05 – 13 Zielgebiete der Stadtentwicklung
STEP 05 – 13 Target Areas for Future Urban Development

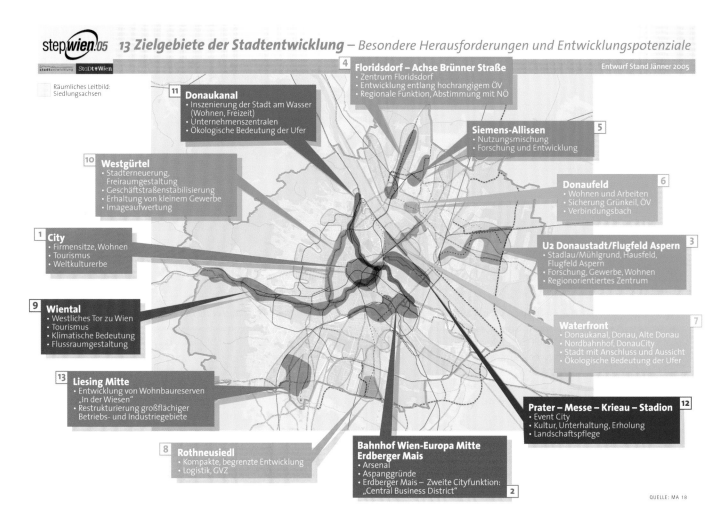

stepwien.05 *13 Zielgebiete der Stadtentwicklung – Besondere Herausforderungen und Entwicklungspotenziale*

Räumliches Leitbild: Siedlungsachsen

4 Floridsdorf – Achse Brünner Straße
· Zentrum Floridsdorf
· Entwicklung entlang hochrangigem ÖV
· Regionale Funktion, Abstimmung mit NÖ

Entwurf Stand Jänner 2005

11 Donaukanal
· Inszenierung der Stadt am Wasser (Wohnen, Freizeit)
· Unternehmenszentralen
· Ökologische Bedeutung der Ufer

5 Siemens-Allissen
· Nutzungsmischung
· Forschung und Entwicklung

10 Westgürtel
· Stadterneuerung, Freiraumgestaltung
· Geschäftsstraßenstabilisierung
· Erhaltung von kleinem Gewerbe
· Imageaufwertung

6 Donaufeld
· Wohnen und Arbeiten
· Sicherung Grünkeil, ÖV
· Verbindungsbach

1 City
· Firmensitze, Wohnen
· Tourismus
· Weltkulturerbe

3 U2 Donaustadt/Flugfeld Aspern
· Stadlau/Mühlgrund, Hausfeld, Flugfeld Aspern
· Forschung, Gewerbe, Wohnen
· Regionorientiertes Zentrum

9 Wiental
· Westliches Tor zu Wien
· Tourismus
· Klimatische Bedeutung
· Flussraumgestaltung

7 Waterfront
· Donaukanal, Donau, Alte Donau
· Nordbahnhof, DonauCity
· Stadt mit Anschluss und Aussicht
· Ökologische Bedeutung der Ufer

13 Liesing Mitte
· Entwicklung von Wohnbaureserven „In der Wiesen"
· Restrukturierung großflächiger Betriebs- und Industriegebiete

12 Prater – Messe – Krieau – Stadion
· Event City
· Kultur, Unterhaltung, Erholung
· Landschaftspflege

8 Rothneusiedl
· Kompakte, begrenzte Entwicklung
· Logistik, GVZ

2 Bahnhof Wien-Europa Mitte Erdberger Mais
· Arsenal
· Aspanggründe
· Erdberger Mais – Zweite Cityfunktion: „Central Business District"

QUELLE: MA 18

Etwa alle zehn Jahre erstellt die Stadt Wien einen Stadtentwicklungsplan, der als strategische Leitlinie für die Verwaltung und für Infrastrukturinvestitionen dient. Im neuen STEP 05 wurden erstmals dreizehn Zielgebiete definiert, für die jeweils konkrete Maßnahmen erarbeitet werden sollen. Prinzipiell lassen sich die Zielgebiete in drei Typen einordnen: strukturbildende Linien wie der Gürtel oder der Donaukanal, Umnutzung älterer Gebiete wie der neue Bahnhof Wien oder die Messe sowie neue Gebiete wie das Flugfeld Aspern.

Zentrales Zielgebiet ist die City, in der sich die Entwicklung in der Polarität zwischen Wirtschafts- und Wohnnutzung sowie dem Tourismus und dem Schutz des Weltkulturerbes darstellen lässt. Einerseits wird der Bebauungsplan in der Innenstadt an den aktuellen Bestand angepasst, also Baurecht vermindert, andererseits wird der Dachausbau gefördert. Einerseits soll der Erlebnischarakter gesteigert und die Fußläufigkeit verbessert, andererseits der öffentliche Raum nicht privatisiert werden.

An die Innenstadt schließt der Donaukanal an, der sich aktuell zu einer Enfilade von Firmensitz-Hochhäusern entwickelt – neuestes Beispiel ist der geplante Doppelturm anstelle des alten Uniqa-Gebäudes – und als neuer Naherholungsraum gehandelt wird, als welcher er allerdings infrastrukturelle Verbesserungen benötigt.

Roughly every ten years the City of Vienna prepares an urban development plan that provides strategic guidelines for the municipal administration and for investment in the infrastructure. The new STEP 05 defines for the first time thirteen target areas, for which concrete measures are to be worked out. Essentially the target areas can be divided into three types: structure-forming trajectories such as the Gürtel ring road or the Danube Canal, older areas to be re-planned such as the new Central Railway Station for Vienna or the Trade Fair Centre, and, thirdly, new areas such as Aspern airfield.

The central target area is the Inner City, where development is positioned in the polarity between business and residential use, between tourism and the conservation of the world cultural heritage. On the one hand the development plan for the inner city is adapted to the current situation, i.e. building rights are curtailed, while on the other the conversion of attic spaces is encouraged. On the one hand the aspect of experiencing the city is to be intensified and the ease of pedestrian accessibility improved, while on the other avoiding the privatisation of public space.

Donaucity   FOTO: MA 21B SVANCAREK

In Verbindung damit steht das Wiental, für das bereits seit Jahren eine so genannte „Renaturierung" in Diskussion ist – abgesehen davon beschränkt sich die Aktualität wohl auf Ausbauten rund ums Schloss Schönbrunn.

Ebenfalls innenstadtnah liegt der Westgürtel, bei dem sich nun die Erfolge des URBAN-Programmes einstellen. Wesentlichster Punkt ist hier der Gaudenzdorfer Knoten, für den es eine ähnliche Ideenfindungsphase wie mit dem Millenniumsworkshop für die KDAG-Gründe geben soll.

Die heißesten Entwicklungsgebiete sind wohl der Bereich Bahnhof Wien-Europa Mitte – Erdberger Mais, die Zone Prater-Messe-Krieau-Stadion entlang der U2-Verlängerung sowie die Waterfront, womit vor allem Donau-City und Nordbahnhof gemeint sind. Auch wenn noch unklar ist, wann mit dem Zentralbahnhofsbau begonnen wird, besitzt dieser Bereich durch die optimale Verkehrsanbindung zumindest mancher dortiger Zonen und die Größe der vorhandenen Flächen viel Potenzial. Der Prater wird durch die U2 unweigerlich aus dem Dornröschenschlaf geweckt. Und in der Donau-City sind etwa zwei Drittel der Fläche bebaut, aber die Realisierung des neuen Masterplans mit Wiens bisher höchsten Hochhäusern steht noch aus – während der Nordbahnhof trotz seiner Größe und Lage seit vielen Jahren dahindämmert.

Im Vergleich dazu sind die übrigen sechs Zielgebiete wohl von eher langfristiger Bedeutung: im Nordosten sind das die Achse Brünnerstraße, Siemens-Allissen und das Donaufeld, alle drei nicht höchstrangig erschlossen, sowie Stadlau und das Flugfeld Aspern, die zwar an der U2 liegen, aber das tut der Nordbahnhof auch. Im Süden sind schließlich Liesing Mitte und Rothneusiedl wohl nicht in unmittelbar nächster Zeit entwicklungsfähig.

The Danube Canal borders the inner city. It is gradually being flanked by a series of company headquarters – the latest example being the twin towers planned to replace the old Uniqa building – and it is also seen as a local recreation area, although to allow it truly function as such improvements to the infrastructure are necessary.

The Wiental (valley of the River Wien) is related to the Canal. For years plans to give this open channel a more „natural" appearance have been discussed – apart from this discussion current plans are restricted to developments around Schönbrunn Palace.

The Westgürtel (western section of the ring-road) is also close to the inner city. The success of the URBAN programme is clearly discernible here. The most important point here is the Gaudenzdorfer Knoten (junction) for which an „ideas phase" is planned, similar to the millennium workshop held for the KDAG site.

The most hotly debated development areas are certainly Bahnhof Wien-Europa Mitte-Erdberger Mais, the Prater-Messe-Krieau-Stadion zone along the extended U2 metro line and the Waterfront, which means by and large the Donau-City and Nordbahnhof (North Railway Station). Even though it is still uncertain when the construction of the new central railway station will start, thanks to the size of the sites available and the optimum transport connections of at least some zones in this district it possesses much potential. The extension of the U2 metro line will inevitably awaken the Prater from its long sleep. In the Donau City around two-thirds of the area available has already been developed, but the realisation of the new master plan, with Vienna's tallest high-rise buildings to date, is still awaited. Finally, despite its size and important location, the Nordbahnhof has been vegetating for many years now.

In comparison to the above areas the other six target areas are all of a more long-term importance. In the northeast these are the Brünnerstrasse axis, Siemens-Allissen and Donaufeld, all three of which are not yet adequately accessed, as well as Stadlau and Aspern airfield, which lie on the U2 (but then so does the Nordbahnhof). In the south the designated areas Liesing Mitte and Rothneusiedl are most probably not developable in the immediate future.

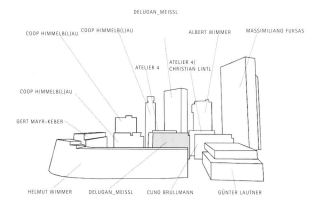

COOP HIMMELB(L)AU COOP HIMMELB(L)AU

DELUGAN_MEISSL

ALBERT WIMMER   MASSIMILIANO FUKSAS

ATELIER 4

ATELIER 4/
CHRISTIAN LINTL

COOP HIMMELB(L)AU

GERT MAYR-KEBER

HELMUT WIMMER   DELUGAN_MEISSL   CUNO BRULLMANN   GÜNTER LAUTNER

Wienerberg City

Wienerberg City

Das Wienerbergareal mit dem Business Park Vienna, dem Twin Tower sowie der eben fertig werdenden Wienerberg City steht für zeitgenössischen Investorenstädtebau. Das Gebiet wurde durch den Baustoffkonzern Wienerberger entwickelt, der die Fläche nicht mehr betrieblich benötigte, insgesamt wurden allein in der Wienerberg City 500 Mio. EUR investiert. Business Park, Twin Tower sowie der BUWOG-Wohnturm gehören Österreichs größtem Immobilienfonds Immofinanz, die hier mit 115.000 m² Fläche ein Drittel seines österreichischen Büroportfolios besitzt. Die Zahlen zeigen allerdings nicht, dass die Wienerberg City mit öffentlichem Verkehr nicht ausreichend erschlossen ist, dass zwar hervorragende Einzelbauten realisiert wurden, aber das städtebauliche Konzept scheinbar nur die maximale Ausnutzung im Blick hatte, und dass als Abgeltung für die Umnutzungsgewinne nur ein Schulgrundstück und ein Kindergarten zur Verfügung gestellt wurden. Nun wird von der öffentlichen Hand verlangt, möglichst bald eine U-Bahnlinie zum Wienerberg zu finanzieren.

Wienerberg City

The Wienerberg area with the Business Park Vienna, the Twin Towers as well as the Wienerberg City now gradually approaching completion is representative of contemporary investor urban development. The area was developed by the Wienerberger building materials company, which no longer required the site for its business. A total of 500 million euro was invested in the Wienerberg City alone. The Business Park, Twin Towers as well as the BUWOG housing tower belong to Austria's largest real estate fund, Immofinanz, which here owns 115,000 m² of office space, a third of its Austrian office portfolio. However, these figures do not reveal that access by public transport to the Wienerberg City is poor, that, although excellent individual buildings have been erected here, the urban development concept seems focussed exclusively on maximum exploitation of space or that, as compensation for the profits made through the rezoning, as yet only a school site and a kindergarten have been provided. Demands have recently been made that the public purse should finance a metro line to Wienerberg as soon as possible.

Donau-City

Die Donau-City ist nicht nur ein Ersatzprojekt für die nicht realisierte Weltausstellung Wien-Budapest 1995, sondern auch Stellvertreter einer langen Reihe von „Wien an die Donau"-Visionen seit der Donauregulierung 1870-75. Und sie steht dadurch, dass einerseits ihr Ort politisch vorgegeben war, durch öffentliche Finanzierung erschlossen wurde und ein Teil der Nutzungen auf politische Entscheidungen zurückgeht, dass sie aber andererseits von einer privaten Gesellschaft realisiert wird, am Übergang zum Investorenstädtebau, wie man ihn heute am Wienerberg und Monte Laa in Reinform sehen kann. Der 1992 von Krischanitz/Neumann entwickelte Masterplan bestand in einer innovativen städtischen Grammatik und schlug eine durchgrünte Stadtlandschaft in den unteren drei Ebenen vor, wurde jedoch faktisch nicht umgesetzt. Nach der Errichtung von Saturn- und Tech-Gate-Tower steht nun die Umsetzung des Perrault-Masterplans an, der aus einem Wettbewerb 2002 hervorging und an die Stelle des alten Peichl-Isozaki-Doppelturmprojektes trat. Perrault sieht zwei etwa 200 Meter hohe Türme sowie einen etwas niedrigeren an der Wagramer Straße vor, weiters plant er am Areal hin zum Donauufer Freizeit-, Veranstaltungs- und Kulturbauten. Welcher Art die Kulturnutzung sein soll und was mit dem der TU Wien gewidmeten Bereich geschehen wird, ist jedoch nach wie vor ungewiss. Neuester Vorschlag ist die Übersiedlung der Universität für angewandte Kunst in ein Coop Himmelb(l)au-Gebäude in der Donau-City.

rt

Donau-City

The Donau-City (Danube City) is not merely a replacement project for the joint Vienna-Budapest World fair originally planned for 1995 but never held. It is also representative of a long series of visions of "Vienna on the Danube" that began with the regulation of the Danube between 1870 and 1875. And, as its location was politically predetermined, access was publicly financed and at least part of the uses were determined at the political level, it represents the transition to investor development, such as can be seen today in its unadulterated form at Wienerberg and Monte Laa. The master plan developed in 1992 by Krischanitz/Neumann used an innovative urban grammar and proposed an urban landscape in which the three lower levels were to be permeated with green space, but was essentially never implemented. After the completion of the Saturn and Tech-Gate towers the implementation of the new Perrault master plan is about to commence. The master plan results from a competition in 2002 replacing the former Peichl-Isozaki twin tower project. Perrault's project includes two towers with 200 metres as well as a lower one at Wagramer Straße. At the waterside he suggests cultural and recreation buildings. Untill now the exact use is unsure as well as the zoning for the Vienna University of Technology. Lately the University of Applied Arts considers to move to Donau-City into a building designed by Coop Himmelb(l)au.

rt

Dominique Perrault:
Masterplan Donau-City

Architektur Consult

T-Center, Wien/Vienna

Photos Paul Ott
Text Matthias Boeckl

Sichtbare Energien

Wiens Umgang mit Stadtbrachen stellt – trotz gestiegenen Entwicklungsdrucks durch die Ostöffnung – keine Geschwindigkeitsweltrekorde auf. Die großen Projekte auf den ehemaligen Bahnhofsterrains verheddern sich im Kleinkrieg mit den Bundesbahnen und selbst die Stadtentwicklungsgebiete im „eigenen" Bereich – wie etwa jenes im Umfeld des bereits vor Jahrzehnten stillgelegten Großschlachthofes St. Marx – wachsen in eher gemächlichem Tempo empor. Droht allerdings das Abwandern eines Großarbeitgebers und -steuerzahlers, dann überstürzen sich die Ereignisse förmlich: In knappen zwei Jahren Bauzeit entstand so das T-Center beim ehemaligen Schlachthofgelände als „größtes Bürogebäude Österreichs".

Visible Energy

Even despite the increased pressure to develop that has resulted from the opening up of Eastern Europe, Vienna's handling of its brownfield sites has not set any world speed records. The major projects on former railway sites are entangled in a battle with the Austrian Federal Railways, and even the urban development areas within the City's „own" area of competence – such as the district around the former St. Marx abattoir, which was closed down years ago – tend to grow at their own rather leisurely pace. If, however, a major employer and taxpayer threatens to relocate its centre of operations then this can precipitate things. In this context the T-Center was erected on the former abattoir site in the space of just two years, as „Austria's largest office building".

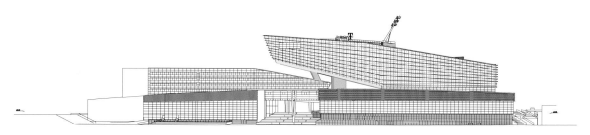

Ansicht Nord-Ost | North-east view

Ansicht Süd-West | South-west view

So läuft das Geschäft

Das T-Center ist ein Lehrstück des real existierenden Städtebaus, nicht nur in Wien. Klopft ein Großinvestor an oder sind gar schon Arbeitsplätze in Gefahr, dann werden oft propagierte hehre Ideale einer nachhaltigen Stadtentwicklung rasch verwässert. Da spielt es plötzlich keine Rolle mehr, ob ein neuer Firmenstandort oder neue Wohnbauten gut an Verkehrswege angebunden sind, eine objektiv messbare Quartierstimulation bieten und die von den Investoren versprochenen Benefits auch tatsächlich geliefert werden. Denn einem Argument von 2.500 Dauerarbeitsplätzen und 220 Millionen Euro Bauinvestitionen, die hier zudem bereits heftig vom regionalen Konkurrenten Niederösterreich umworben waren, kann man eben nur wenig entgegen setzen. Da wünscht man sich lieber in die souveräne Position des Bauwerbers als in jene der Stadtverwaltung, die hier, wenn sie schon nicht, wie es Günther Domenig ironisch formulierte, dem Projekt die Genehmigungen förmlich „nachgeworfen hat", sich doch zumindest „kooperativ" verhalten musste (Hermann Eisenköck). Immerhin hatte sie ja aus Angst vor der Abwanderung des Großarbeitgebers selbst das Zustandekommen eines Bauherrenkonsortiums initiiert, das aus zwei Banken und einer großen Versicherung geschmiedet und vom erfahrenen Manager des Donaucity-Developers geleitet wurde. Der gerühmte „Investor" T-Mobile und T-Systems ist in Wahrheit nur der Nutzer, der nicht mehr als „marktübliche Mieten" (Hermann Eisenköck) zahlen, aber einen guten Standort irgendwo in der Region haben wollte – und das könnte, so lautet die kaum verhüllte Drohung, neben Wien ebenso gut auch Niederösterreich, Bratislava oder Györ sein. Die herzeigbare Architektur nahm man dankend in Kauf (T-Mobile Chef Pölzl meinte gnädig, bei gleichem Mietpreis sei ein Architekturstatement wohl einem hässlichen Bau vorzuziehen) und ließ sich ansonsten ein Gebäude nach Maß von einem Bauherren bauen, der damit die auf 15 Jahre abgeschlossene Vermietung seines Hauses sicherstellte. Ummittelbar nach dessen Errichtung und Vermietung an T-Mobile und T-Systems wurde es – gemeinsam mit dem „Saturn-Tower" der Wiener Donaucity – folgerichtig und einträglich um 380 Millionen Euro an einen internationalen Immobilieninvestor verkauft. So und nicht anders funktioniert heute die Planung und Verwertung städtebaulich relevanter Großprojekte.

How Business Really is

The T-Center is an instructive example of the real state of urban development – and not just in Vienna. If a major investor knocks on the door, or if jobs are threatened then noble ideals of sustainable urban development often propagated are quickly watered down. Suddenly it is of little importance whether a new company location or new housing blocks are well connected to the transport system, whether they offer objectively quantifiable stimulation for a district, or whether the benefits promised by the investors are actually delivered. There is, after all, little that can be said against the argument of 2,500 permanent jobs and an investment in construction of 220 million Euro, both of which in this case were eagerly sought after by a regional competitor, the province of Lower Austria. It is infinitely preferable to find oneself in the sovereign position of the applicant for planning permission rather than in that of the city administration which, while it may not have, as Günther Domenig ironically put it, formally „thrown the planning approval at the project", was at least obliged to behave „cooperatively" (Hermann Eisenköck). After all, out of fear that a major employer would leave the region the municipal authorities themselves had initiated the establishment of a client consortium consisting of two banks and a large insurance company that was directed by the experienced manager of the Donau City developer. The vaunted „investor", T-mobile and T-Systems, is, in fact, only a user who pays nothing more than the usual market rent (Hermann Eisenköck), but who wanted to have a good location somewhere in the region– which, according to the scarcely veiled threat, could equally well be in Lower Austria, Bratislava or Györ, as in Vienna. The presentable architecture was gratefully accepted (T-Mobile boss Pölzl said gracefully that, for the same rent, an architectural statement is preferable to an ugly building) and a made-to-measure building was erected by a developer, who was thus able to ensure a 15-year letting for his building. Directly after constructing the building and letting it to T-Mobile and T-Systems, it was logically and lucratively sold for 380 million Euro to an international real estate investor, along with the „Saturn Tower" in the Vienna Donau-City. This (and no differently) is how the planning and utilization of major projects of urban relevance are carried out nowadays.

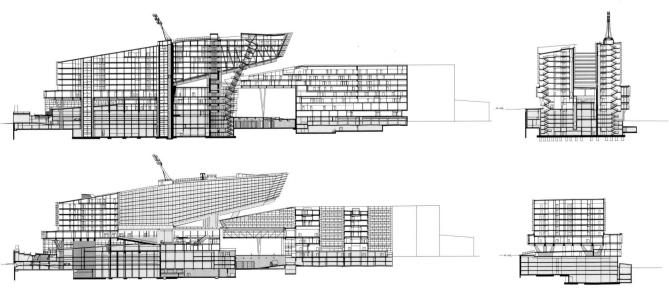

Schiffsrumpf über Stadtgewusel

Unter diesen Bedingungen ist gelungene Architektur wohl ein seltener Ausnahmefall, der von geschickten Spielern hinter den Kulissen, wie zweifellos Hermann Eisenköck einer ist, mit persönlichen Beziehungen erst sorgfältig eingefädelt werden muss. Das ist die smarte österreichische Variante des ansonsten eher desillusionierenden globalen Immobiliengeschäfts und in Wien trat dieser Glücksfall auch tatsächlich ein, denn sowohl die lokal gegebene Verkehrsinfrastruktur als auch die Ziele der Stadtentwicklung rund um St. Marx und die Qualität der Architektur standen in einem einigermaßen günstigen Verhältnis zueinander. Zwei Unternehmen und sieben Wiener Standorte des in Österreich rasch gewachsenen größten deutschen Telekommunikationsanbieters sollten unter einem Dach zusammengeführt werden, was für das gewaltige Volumen von 134.000 m² Bruttogeschoßfläche sorgte. Doch nicht bloß Büroflächen, sondern auch vermietbare Läden, soziale Einrichtungen, ein weithin sichtbares Signal sowie einen städtebaulichen Zündfunken für das Entwicklungsgebiet St. Marx wollte man hier schaffen. Dieses Gebiet ist mit (Flughafen-)Schnellbahn, Straßenbahn und Autobahn in unmittelbarer Nähe gut erschlossen – eine Chance, die man jedoch durch weitsichtige Detailplanung (besonders für Autozufahrten und Fußgängerverbindungen zu den Öffis) wesentlich besser hätte nutzen können. So tritt das schon vom Museumsquartier her bekannte Paradoxon ein, dass eine Großinstitution in bester Lage nur über Hürden erreicht werden kann.

Das Terrain fällt vom Rennweg, entlang dessen sich der hoch aufragende Schiffsrumpf in Richtung Stadtautobahn erstreckt, zum ehemaligen Schlachthofgelände hin ab, was den Architekten Anlass für eine schöne Freiraumgestaltung mit Rampen, Treppen und Wegen unter den aufgestelzten Haupttrakten des Gebäudes bot. Der gewaltige Baukörper ist in mehrere Elemente aufgelöst, vor allem einen Kamm mit zwei Paralleltrakten und eine große Zackenform, die sich nach Osten hin zu jenem spitzwinkligen Rumpf auftürmt, der den Wienern bereits ein vertrautes und beliebtes Fortschrittssymbol am Wegesrande ihrer täglichen Quälerei über die chronisch verstopfte, in Hochlage verlaufende Stadtautobahn „Südwesttangente" geworden ist. In unmittelbarer Nachbarschaft zum T-Center befinden sich die denkmalgeschützten historischen Rinderhallen des ehemaligen Schlachthofes. Gemeinsam mit dem angrenzenden Terrain des rasch expandierenden Vienna Biocenter könnte so im ehemaligen Hinterhof der Stadt tatsächlich bald ein pulsierendes, durchmischtes Quartier entstehen. Dazu bedarf es freilich noch zahlreicher weiterer, gut überlegter Neuansiedlungen verschiedenster Nutzung, die dann endlich auch die immer noch fehlenden Wohnungen, Supermärkte, kleinen Läden und Kindergärten bringen müssten.

A Ship's Hull above the Urban Throng

Under such circumstances successful architecture is a rare exception that must be carefully negotiated behind the scenes by adroit players, one of whom Hermann Eisenköck most certainly is. That is the smart Austrian variation of the otherwise rather disillusioning global real estate business and in Vienna this stroke of luck did in fact occur, for both the existing transport infrastructure as well as the goals of urban development around St. Marx and the quality of the architecture were in a reasonably favourable relationship to each other. Two businesses and seven Viennese locations of the largest German telecommunications provider that has grown rapidly in Austria were to be combined under a single roof, which meant an enormous gross floor area of 134,000 m². But the aim here was not just to create office space but also rentable shops, social amenities, and a signal visible from afar, as well as an urban ignition spark for the St. Marx development area. This area is well connected in transport terms with the (airport) railway line, trams and a motorway connection in close proximity – yet this opportunity could have been better exploited by devoted detail planning (in particular of the approach roads and pedestrian connections to the public transport system). And so a paradox that we are familiar with from the Vienna Museumsquartier cropped up again here: that apparently a large institution in an excellent location can be reached only by crossing a number of obstacles.

The site falls from Rennweg, along which the soaring ship's hull stretches in the direction of the city motorway, to the former abattoir grounds – a situation that offered the architects the chance to produce a fine design of external space with ramps, staircases and paths under the elevated main body of the building. The mighty body of the building is broken up into several elements, above all a comb with two parallel wings and a large jagged form that rises eastwards to form the angular hull that has already become a familiar and popular symbol of progress for the Viennese that they see during their daily ordeal on the chronically congested elevated urban motorway, the so-called „Südosttangente". The historic cattle sheds of the former abattoir, which are protected buildings, are in the immediate neighbourhood of the T-Center. Together with the adjoining site of the rapidly expanding Vienna Biocenter there is now a concrete possibility that a pulsating and well-mixed district could develop here in a former backyard of the city. Naturally, to achieve this goal it is necessary to locate numerous further, well-considered new developments with very diverse functions here, which would finally bring with them the apartments, supermarkets, small shops and kindergartens that are still lacking.

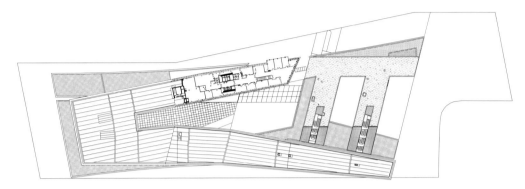

11. Obergeschoß | 11th level

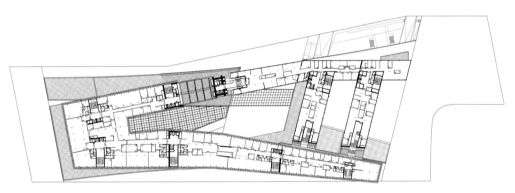

4. Obergeschoß | 4th level

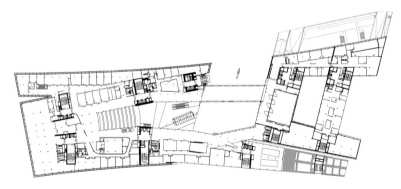

2. Obergeschoß | 2nd level

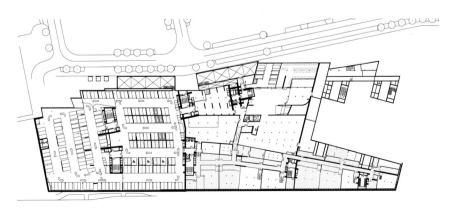

4. Untergeschoß | 4th basement

Empfangshalle | Lobby

Ästhetisierung des Bedrohlichen?

Das T-Center selbst ist eher Geste als lebendiger Stadtbestand-teil, da neben den Büros große Volumensteile einem gewal-tigen Rechenzentrum ohne jedes Anzeichen irdischen Lebens überlassen sind. Paradoxerweise wird aber selbst diese Wüste an mietbaren Bits und Bytes zum Argument für die Stadtver-träglichkeit des Projekts, denn „mit dem T-Center-Rechenzen-trum begegnen wir dem internationalen Trend zur Absiedlung von Rechenzentren und sind damit als Outsourcing-Partner für österreichische Unternehmen exzellent gerüstet. Gerade bei der Auswahl des Outsourcing-Partners spielen die Aspek-te Sicherheit und lokale Präsenz eine wesentliche Rolle", so der Boss von T-Systems, die von hier aus bereits 100 Firmen IT-mäßig betreut und in zehn europäischen Ländern aktiv ist. Die Büros selbst – vorwiegend als großzügige Großraumbüros geplant, aber rasch der dumpfen Realverfassung österreichi-scher Arbeitsplätze angepasst – bieten außer ihrer jeweils mehr oder weniger spektakulären Lage kaum Innovatives. Elegant ist hingegen die zentrale Halle mit ihrer breiten Rampe in die Obergeschoße, die allerdings für Zufallsbesucher oder Stadtfla-neure off limits ist.

Günther Domenig, der innerhalb der erfolgreichen Planerfirma „Architektur Consult" vor allem für die Großform ihrer Bauten zuständig war, spricht da lieber vom „Tomahawk", den das Haus in den städtischen Himmel über Wien zeichnet, Hans Hollein vom „liegenden Wolkenkratzer", der hier Beachtung verdie-ne. Abgesehen von derlei süffigen Metaphern ist das T-Center tatsächlich ein klar lesbares Konzentrat jener wirtschaftlichen und technischen Energien, die sonst oft im Verborgenen unsere Städte formen und hier demonstrativ präsentiert werden. Eine Ästhetisierung des Bedrohlichen? Jedenfalls wissen wir nun, aus welchem Material zeitgenössischer Städtebau gemacht ist, in jeder Beziehung.

Aesthetically Disguising a Threat?

The T-Center itself is more of a gesture than a living part of the city, as, in addition to the offices, large parts of its volume are given up to a huge data processing centre without any visible sign of earthly life. Paradoxically, even this desert of rentable bits and bytes becomes an argument for the urban compatibility of the project because „with the T-Center data processing centre we confront the international trend to relocate such centres and are therefore excellently equipped as an outsourcing partner for Austrian businesses. In choosing an outsourcing partner it is precisely the aspects of security and local presence that play an important role", according to the boss of T-Systems that from this base already provides in-formation technology services to 100 companies and is active in ten European countries. The offices themselves – mostly planned as large open plan offices but rapidly adapted to conform with the dull reality of Austrian workplaces – offer hardly anything innovative, apart from their more or less spectacular location. In contrast the central hall with its broad ramp leading to the upper floors – which, incidentally, is off-limits for casual visitors or urban strollers – is most elegant.

Günther Domenig, who was responsible for the overall form of the building within the extremely successfully planning firm „Architektur Consult", prefers to talk in this context of a „tomahawk", that the building describes in the urban sky over Vienna, while Hans Hollein speaks of a „recumbent skyscrap-er" that is deserving of recognition. Apart from such pleasant metaphors the T-Center is in fact a clearly legible concentrate of the economic and technical energies that often shape our cities secretly, but which here are demonstratively presented. An aesthetic treatment of something essentially threatening? Whatever the case, now we know the material contemporary urban planning is made of – in every sense.

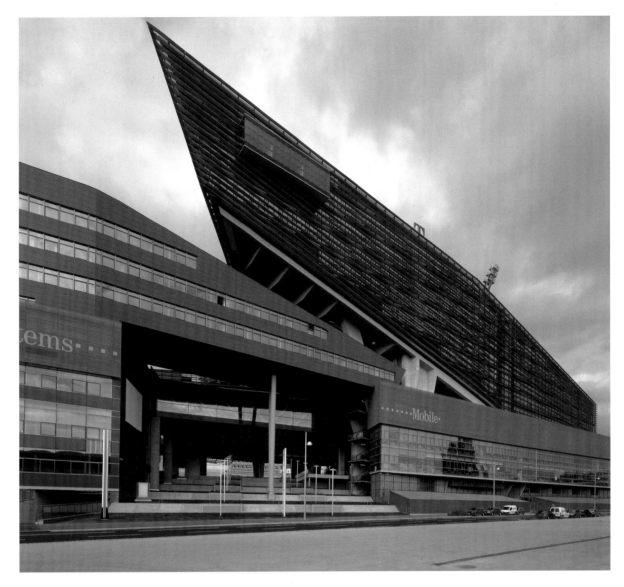

T-Center
Wien-St. Marx, Rennweg 97-99

Bauherr I client **MM Liegenschaftsbesitz GmbH**
Generalunternehmer I building contractor **PORR AG, Wien; WIBEBA GmbH, Wien**
Planung I planning **Architektur Consult – Domenig Eisenköck Peyker**
Projektleitung I project manager **DDipl. Ing. Christian Halm**
Mitarbeiter I assistance **Thomas Schwed; Michael Bieglmayer, Martin Flatz, Helmut Frötscher, Sandra Harrich,**
    Gregor Kassl, Markus Klausecker, Karin Köberl, Jan Kokol, Patrick Krähenbühl, Birgit Krizek, Alexander Kunz,
    Peter Liaunig, Robert Mölzer, Elke Nicolaus, Gerhard Pfeiler, Nicole Rumpler, Katharina Schneiter, Hannes
    Schwed, Roland Thierrichter, Oliver Ulrich, Ralf Wanek, Johannes Weigl, Heribert Wolfmayr, Rainer Wührer
Statik I structural consultant **Wendl ZT GmbH, Graz; Vasko + Partner GesmbH, Wien**
Fassaden/Fenster I facade/windows **Alu-Sommer, Stoob; MCE, Linz**
Dach I roof **ISO-Bau, Wien**
Dachbahnen I roofing membrane **Sarnafil T/Haberkorn GmbH, Wolfurt**
Mauerwerk I masonry **PORR – WIBEBA, Wien**
Türen I doors **MBS, Weitensfeld; STEBA, Ottnang**
Trockenbau I dry structure **Lindner, Baden; Schreiner, Graz**
Elektroinstallationen I electrical services **VA Tech Elin, Wien**
Sanitäre Installationen I plumbing **Ortner, Wien**
Abscheidetechnik/Hebeanlagen I drainage systems/pump station **ACO Passavant, Baden**
Heizung/Lüftung/Klima I heating/ventilation/air conditioning **BACON, Wien**
Lichtplanung/-ausstattung I lighting concept/fittings **Zumtobel Staff, Dornbirn/Wien**
Böden I flooring **Lindner, Baden; Kampichler, Wr. Neustadt**
Möbel I furnishings **Bene, Wien; Neudörfler, Wien; Kirchberger, Linz**
Wandverkleidung I panelling **3-Stern, Wien**
Aufzug I elevators **Thyssen, Wien**

Grundstücksfläche I site area	27.000 m²
Nutzfläche I floor area	119.000 m²
Bebaute Fläche I built-up area	15.000 m²
Umbauter Raum I cubage	550.000 m³
Planungsbeginn I start of planning	1/2000
Baubeginn I start of construction	2/2002
Fertigstellung I completion	7/2004
Baukosten I building costs	220 Mio EUR

Boris Podrecca

Vienna Biocenter 2

Photos Gerald Zugmann
Text Matthias Boeckl

Top-Notch Research

Der Stadtteil St. Marx, eine der größten Industriebrachen Wiens rund um den ehemaligen Schlachthof, ist ein wichtiges Hoffnungsgebiet der Stadtentwicklung. Vor einigen Jahren wurde hier – einen Steinwurf vom T-Center entfernt – der Bau des Vienna Biocenter in Angriff genommen, das nun auf den umliegenden Flächen rasch expandieren und Wien eine wichtige Stellung im extrem kompetitiven internationalen Wissenschaftsgeschäft sichern soll.

Top-Notch Research

The city district of St. Marx, one of Vienna's largest industrial brownfield areas centred on a former abattoir, is a district where hopes for future urban development are focussed. Some years ago, only a stone's throw from the T-Center, development of the Vienna Biocenter has started, which is planned to expand rapidly across the surrounding area and is intended to secure for Vienna an important place in the extremely competitive international science business.

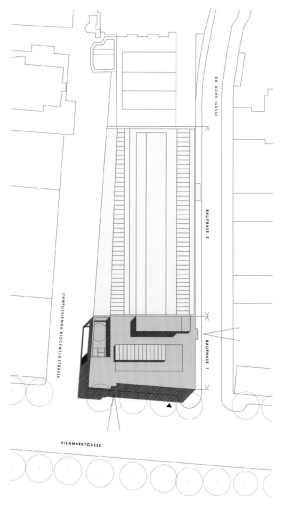

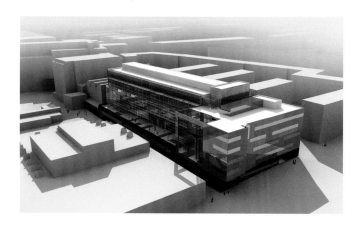

Das Wissens-Geschäft

Biologie ist heute eine heiß umkämpfte Disziplin, in der die Forschung Millioneninvestitionen verarbeitet und die Industrie Milliardenbeträge an Wertschöpfung erwirtschaftet. Längst sind die beschaulichen Zeiten vorbei, als Wissenschafter um der reinen akademischen Ehre willen an ihren Reagenzgläsern arbeiteten. Die Wertschöpfungskette ist heute räumlich dicht aneinandergerückt und auch in Wien wollte man Forscher, Lehrende, Studierende und vor allem die Verwertungsindustrie unter einem Dach zusammen bringen. Um in diesem globalen Megageschäft auch nur einen winzigen Standortvorteil gegenüber den großen Forschungsfabriken in Asien und Amerika zu erarbeiten, bedarf es jedoch geballter Forschungs- und Investorenkraft. Für das Vienna Biocenter 2 verbündeten sich die Österreichische Akademie der Wissenschaften, der Pharmakonzern Boehringer Ingelheim und die Stadt Wien, um in einem Public Private Partnership über einen privaten Developer die entsprechende Infrastruktur zu schaffen. An Partnern konnte man bereits mehrere Biotechnologiefirmen und Universitätsinstitute gewinnen, die hier ihre Zelte aufschlugen, aber vor allem den jungen Wissenschafts-Superstar Josef Penninger, der im zweiten Bauteil des Vienna Biocenter sein top-notch Institute of Molecular Biotechnology (IMBA) beziehen wird. Die Auspizien dieser Konstellation stehen also relativ günstig für das angestrebte Durchstarten einer neuen, kommerziell orientierten Wiener Biotechnologie von Weltklasse. Rundum stehen Brachen und abrissreife Altbauten zur raschen Expansion zur Verfügung, um den Kern des Biocenter mit weiteren Labor-, Büro- und Wohnbauten zu einem regelrechten Biocampus erweitern und damit einen global ernst zu nehmenden Cluster schaffen zu können.

The Business of Science

Biology today is a hotly contested discipline where research facilities demand investments of many millions and industry generates billions in added value. Those simple days when scientists worked with their test tubes for the sake of academic prestige alone are long past. The links on the chain of added value are today spatially densely packed and in Vienna too the desire crystallized to bring researchers, teachers, students and, above all, the industry that processes their knowledge under a single roof. In order to achieve even a minimal location advantage over the large research factories in Asia and America it is essential to concentrate the combined strengths of researchers and investors. For the Vienna Biocenter 2 the Austrian Academy of Sciences joined forces with the pharmaceuticals company Boehringer Ingelheim and the City of Vienna to create the requisite infrastructure by means of a public private partnership, using a private developer. It proved possible to persuade several biology technology companies and university institutes to make their home here – above all the young scientist superstar, Josef Penninger, who will establish his top-notch Institute of Molecular Biotechnology (IMBA) in the second development phase of the Vienna Biocenter. The auspices of this constellation therefore seem relatively favourable for the goal of rapidly establishing a new, commercially oriented Viennese biotechnology centre of a world-class standard. The new centre is surrounded by brownfield sites and old buildings ripe for demolition that offer space for the rapid expansion of the core of the Biocenter by adding further laboratory, office and residential buildings with the goal of creating a proper bio campus and a cluster that will merit serious attention on the global scale.

VIENNA BIO CENTER
CAMPUS VIENNA BIO CENTER 2
IDENT VIEHMARKTGASSE 2A

Biocenter 2: Bauteil 1 | 1st building

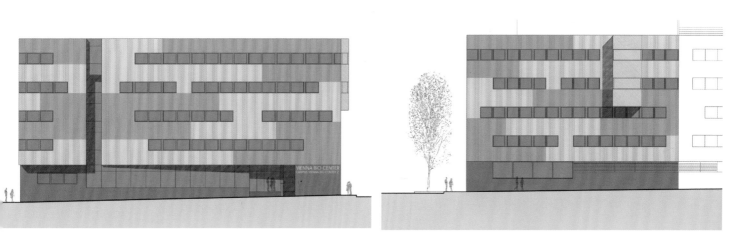

Autistische Labors

Boris Podreccas Projekt ging aus einem EU-weiten Wettbewerb unter dem Juryvorsitzenden Zvi Hecker hervor, der erste Bauteil, in dem vor allem Laborräume untergebracht sind, ist nun in Betrieb, der zweite bereits fertig gestellt. Das architektonische Kernproblem solcher Laborbauten ist zweifellos die schwierige Verbindung seiner hermetisch abgeschotteten Arbeitsräume mit der Außenwelt. Die Herausforderung besteht darin, einem autistisch eingebunkerten Betrieb und seinem Personal Ansätze osmotischen Verhaltens gegenüber ihrer Umwelt räumlich zumindest zu ermöglichen, was vor allem durch eine zentrale Halle erreicht wird. Diese gebäudehohe Halle ist rundum von Laubengängen erschlossen, aus denen Ausbuchtungen in den inneren Luftraum ragen. Diese Kommunikationsinseln sind typisch für den labordominierten Forschungsbetrieb – einerseits können sie für den Austausch in Arbeitspausen genutzt werden, andererseits muss für Besprechungen niemand mehr das streng geheime Labor jemandes anderen betreten. Podrecca löst diese interessante Aufgabe mit der ihm eigenen Formen- und Farbenvielfalt. Jede Ebene der Laubengänge hat eine andere Bodenfarbe, die Balkons der Kommunikationsinseln sind versetzt angeordnet, sodass sich in ihrer Ansicht abwechslungsreiche geometrische Rahmenmuster ausbilden, ihre Verglasungen sind in drei verschiedenen Tönen gehalten. Aber nicht nur die innere Kommunikationszone zählt zu den gestaltbaren Bereichen eines Laborbaus. Auch die Fassade kann als Schnittstelle zur Realität draußen interpretiert werden. Podrecca wählte für den ersten Bauteil, den die Stadt Wien gemeinsam mit dem Developer „Prisma" errichtete, die Teilung in einen Sockel- und einen oberen Bereich. Sein ausgeprägtes Materialsensorium führt ihn zu immer neuen Experimenten und wir erfahren hier, dass eloxiertes Alubech in Zick-Zack-Profil eine ebenso elegante Erscheinung abgeben kann wie der chinesische Basalt der Sockelzone.

Autistic Laboratories

Boris Podrecca's project was selected by a jury chaired by Zvi Hecker in a competition that was open to entrants from throughout the EU. The first building element that accommodates mostly laboratories is already in operation, and the second building has just recently been completed. The central architectural problem of such laboratory buildings is, without any doubt, the difficulty of connecting the hermetically detached workspaces with the exterior world. The challenge lies in providing spatial conditions that at least allow an autistically isolated operation and its staff to develop the rudiments of osmotic behaviour towards their environment. This challenge was met here by the use of a central hall. This hall extends the full height of the building and is surrounded on all sides by circulation decks that at places bulge out into the central void. These "communication islands" are typical of the laboratory-dominated research business – on the one hand they can be used during breaks for the exchange of ideas, on the other hand no one any longer has to enter somebody else's strictly secret laboratory to discuss something. Podrecca solves this interesting challenge with his individual diversity of forms and colours. Each deck level has a differently coloured floor, the balconies of the "communication islands" are staggered in relation to each other so that when viewed from the front they create a varied geometric pattern, and they are glazed is in three different shades. But the communications zones are not the only area of a laboratory building where design can be applied. The façade can be interpreted as an interface to the exterior reality. For the first building phase, which the City of Vienna erected jointly with the developer "Prisma", Podrecca divided the building into a plinth and an upper area. His highly developed sensitivity for materials constantly leads him to new experiments and here he shows us that anodised aluminium sheeting with a zigzag profile can create just as elegant an appearance as the Chinese basalt that he used for the plinth zone.

Bauteil 1: Zentrale Halle mit Laubengang-Fassaden | 1st building: Central hall with circulation decks

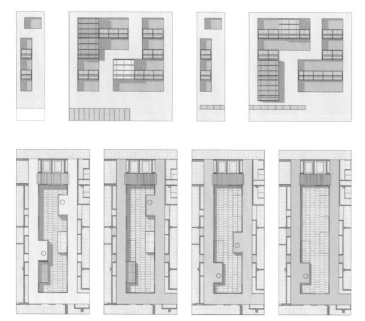

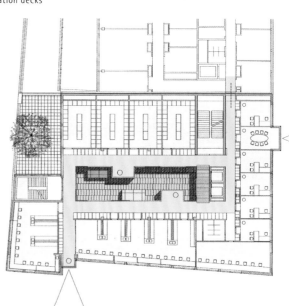

Bauteil 1+2 | 1st and 2nd building

Städtebauliche Bedeutung

Diese Sockelzone zieht sich in den zweiten Bauteil weiter, den die Akademie der Wissenschaften gemeinsam mit Boehringer Ingelheim errichtete und verbindet damit die beiden unmittelbar benachbarten Projekte zu einer visuellen Einheit. Auch die Gänge im Inneren werden vom Kopfbau in den zweiten Bauteil weiter gezogen und münden dort in eine große Halle mit angenehm sanft ansteigenden Treppen und einem gläsernen Lift, welche die Haupterschließung der regalartigen Gebäudestruktur übernimmt. Die Eigenheiten eines Laborgebäudes mit seiner fast übergroßen Bedeutung der Fassade hatten für den hier aktiven Pharmahersteller Boehringer Ingelheim bereits früher die Architekten Sauerbruch/Hutton im deutschen Biberach zu bewältigen (*architektur.aktuell* 3/2003). Die Fassade des zweiten Bauteils des Vienna Biocenter 2 zeigt neben den Basaltplatten (die farblich unterschiedlich in Feinschliff, geflammt und mit Sandstrahl bearbeitet sind) auch emaillierte Glasplatten in unterschiedlichen Grün- und Gelbtönen, was auch als Anspielung auf die Biowissenschaften des Hauses verstanden werden kann. Auch Fotodrucke molekularer Strukturen auf Folie zwischen Verbundgläsern signalisieren über dem Haupteingang die hier bearbeiteten Aufgaben. Gemeinsam mit einer Rotbuche, die an der Rückseite des ersten Bauteils auf der Terrasse über dem Gebäudesockel wächst, vermitteln Podreccas Texturen und verschiedenartige Oberflächen der eher kalten Laborwelt immerhin einen gewissen Charme und eine nicht alltägliche Eleganz, die angesichts der hier verarbeiteten Investitionen und der weit reichenden Bedeutung des in Zukunft hoffentlich hier Entdeckten jede Legitimation besitzt. Die in der Umgebung angestrebten Erweiterungen zum Forschungscampus machen auch städtebaulich im Zusammenhang mit dem nahen T-Center, den Veranstaltungsorten der „Arena", neuen Wohnbauten und der generellen Aufwertung des ehemaligen, eher unschönen Industriequartiers viel Sinn.

Significance for Urban Planning

This plinth zone is continued in the second building, which the Austrian Academy of Sciences erected jointly with Boehringer Ingelheim and thus it connects two directly neighbouring projects to form a single visual entity. The internal corridors are also continued from the end of the first building into the second building, where they terminate in a large hall with pleasantly shallow staircases and a glazed lift that represents the main circulation system for the shelf-like structure of the building. Combining the individual qualities of a laboratory building with the almost excessive significance of the façade is a task architects Sauerbruch Hutton have already handled for the same company, the pharmaceuticals manufacturer Boehringer Ingelheim, in Biberach, Germany (*architektur.aktuell* 3/2003). In addition to the basalt slabs (that are sandblasted, finely polished and differ in colour) the façade of the second part of the Vienna Biocenter 2 has enamelled glass panels in different shades of green and yellow, which could be understood as a reference to the biological sciences to which the building is devoted. Photographic prints of molecular structures set in laminated glass panes are positioned at particular points in the façade and signalise the work that goes on here. Together with a red beech growing at the rear of the first building on the terrace above the plinth, Podrecca's textures and various surfaces lend the somewhat cold laboratory world a certain charm and an uncommon elegance that, in view of the investments that are processed here and the wide-ranging significance of the discoveries that will hopefully be made in the future, is entirely legitimate. The efforts being made to develop the surroundings into a research campus in conjunction with the nearby T-Center, the "Arena" premises for cultural events, new housing developments and the general improvements to what was once a rather ugly industrial district also make a great deal of sense in terms of urban planning.

Vienna Biocenter 2
Wien-St. Marx, Campus Vienna

Bauherr | client **Competence Investment AG, Dornbirn**
Planung | planning **Boris Podrecca**
Projektleitung | project manager **Gerhard Hagelkrüys**
Mitarbeiter | assistance **Hannes Zerlauth, Sibel Anil**
Visualisierungen | visualizations **www.beyer.co.at, studiobaff.com, Roman Bönsch**
Statik | structural consultant **Fröhlich & Locher ZT GmbH**
Elektro-/Sanitärplanung | electrical/plumbing concept **Von der Heyden GmbH**
Planung Heizung/Lüftung/Klima | heating/ventilation/air conditioning concept **Käferhaus GmbH**
Fassaden | facade **Wieser GmbH, Zeltweg; LWZ Luzia & Wolfgang Zorn**
Dach | roof **Ferroglas Glasbautechnik GmbH**
Mauerwerk | masonry **MID-Bau GmbH**
Fenster | windows **Franz Kreuzroither Metallbau GmbH & Co KG**
Portal-/Gewichtschlosser | portal/metalwork **Alu-Stahl Berger GmbH**
Trockenbau | dry construction **Schreiner**
Elektroinstallationen | electrical services **Csernohorszky GmbH**
Heizung/Lüftung/Klima/Sanitäre Installationen | heating/ventilation/air conditioning/plumbing
    August Lengauer GmbH
Aufzug | elevators **Schindler Aufzüge**

Grundstücksfläche | site area	1.121 m²
Nutzfläche | floor area	3.400 m²
Bebaute Fläche | built-up area	1.121 m²
Umbauter Raum | cubage	28.000 m³
Planungsbeginn | start of planning	7/2001
Baubeginn | start of construction	5/2002
Fertigstellung | completion	12/2003
Baukosten | building costs	7 Mio EUR
Kosten pro m² | cost per m²	980,– EUR

Anton Schweighofer

Geriatriezentrum im Kaiser-Franz-Josef-Spital, Wien-Favoriten
Geriatric Care Centre in Kaiser-Franz-Josef-Spital, Vienna-Favoriten

Photos Anna Blau
Text Christian Kühn

Haus als Stadt und Haus als Baum

Als die Gemeinde Wien 1996 einen Wettbewerb für die Planung eines geriatrischen Zentrums im Kaiser-Franz-Josef-Spital ausschrieb, ging es nicht nur um 240 neue Pflegeplätze, sondern auch um die Suche nach einem neuen Bautyp. Eine Geriatrie ist weder Krankenhaus noch Altenheim, sondern eine Mischung beider Bauaufgaben. Im Idealfall gelingt in dieser Institution eine „reaktivierende" Pflege, also das Aufrechterhalten von Lebensfreude im Angesicht und im Bewusstsein des unvermeidlich Brüchigen jeder Existenz. Das beste räumliche Umfeld dafür ist die kleine, überschaubare Einheit, möglichst nicht isoliert vom Rest der Welt, sondern eingebettet in eine vielfältige und lebendige Umgebung.

House as City and House as Tree

When the municipal authority of Vienna set up a competition for the planning of a geriatric care centre in the Kaiser Franz Josef Spital (hospital) in 1996 the initial requirement was not only to provide 240 new care beds but also to discover a new building type. A geriatric care centre is neither a hospital nor a home for the elderly but a "cross" between these two types of building. In the ideal case such an institution can offer "reactivating" care, i.e. a certain joy in living can be maintained despite and in full awareness of the fragility of each human existence. The best spatial setting for such a facility is a small, manageable unit, as far as possible not isolated from the rest of the world but embedded in varied and lively surroundings.

Die „soziale Kunst"

Die Ökonomie des Gesundheitswesens gibt freilich Parameter vor, mit denen sich solche Ideale nicht direkt umsetzen lassen: hohe Dichte, niedrige Baukosten, effizienter Betrieb. Im konkreten Fall bedeutete das eine Bruttogeschoßfläche von 35.000 m², wobei neben den Bettenstationen auch eine Großküche für das gesamte Franz-Josef-Spital zu errichten war. Anton Schweighofer hat mit seinem Projekt eine Annäherung an das Ideal der überschaubaren, ins städtische Umfeld eingebetteten Pflege versucht: Er orientiert sich in Höhenentwicklung und Orientierung des Hauptbaukörpers nicht am Pavillonsystem des bestehenden Krankenhauses, sondern an der angrenzenden Wohnbebauung. Zugleich konzipiert er die Geriatrie im Inneren als feingliedriges städtisches Netzwerk, als Abfolge von Wegen und Plätzen mit raffinierten Abstufungen von privaten und öffentlichen Zonen.

Das Verhältnis zwischen Individuum und Gesellschaft – ein Thema, das Schweighofer in seiner Architektur schon immer in den Mittelpunkt gerückt hat – erfährt unter den Bedingungen eines Pflegeheims besondere Brisanz. Schweighofer ist von allen Architekten, die je mit Architektur als einer „sozialen Kunst" assoziiert wurden, wahrscheinlich jener, dem die Autonomie des Individuums das größte Anliegen ist. Sein Idealbild vom Wohnen lässt sich am besten mit einem Ein-Mann-Zelt vergleichen: eine individuelle Grundeinheit, passgenau um den flexiblen Menschen geschneidert, aber mit freien Valenzen nach außen, sodass sich rundum immer wieder neue soziale Felder aufspannen lassen. Realisiert hat Schweighofer diese Idee beispielsweise in einem Studentenheim in Wien-Favoriten, wo jeder Bewohner über eine Zelle mit 2,3 mal 2,8 m verfügt, die in einem gemeinsam nutzbaren Großraum frei aufgestellt ist.

The "Social Art"

The economic restraints of the public health system dictate parameters that do not allow such ideals to be achieved directly: high-density, low building costs and efficient operational systems are called for nowadays. In this specific case this meant a total floor area of 35,000 square metres, whereby in addition to the bed stations a large kitchen for the entire Franz Josef Spital was also to be built. In his project Anton Schweighofer developed an approach to a kind of care system that is small-scale and embedded in the urban environment. In the height and orientation of the main building block he does not refer to the pavilion system of the existing hospital but rather to the adjoining housing blocks of the city. At the same time he designs the interior of the geriatric care centre as a finely articulated urban network, a sequence of routes and squares with subtly demarcated private and public zones. The relationship between the individual and society – a theme that has always occupied a central role in Schweighofer's architecture – acquires a certain edge in the context of a nursing home. Of all the architects associated with architecture as a "social art" Schweighofer is probably the one for whom the autonomy of the individual is of greatest importance. His ideal notion of living is best represented by a one-man tent: an individual basic unit that is tailored precisely to suit the flexible human being but with enough surplus material on the outside to allow new social fields to be spanned around it. Schweighofer realised this idea in a student residence in Vienna-Favoriten where each resident has a cell measuring 2.3 by 2.8 meters that is freely placed within a communally used large space.

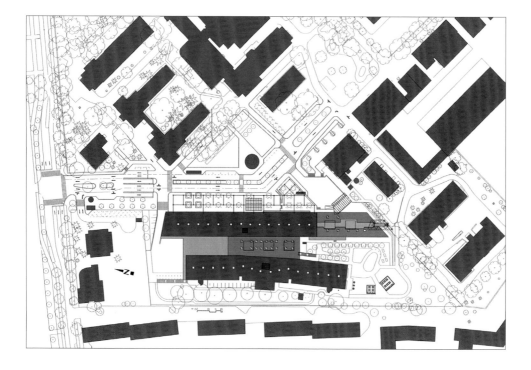

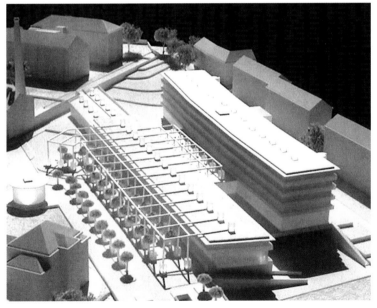

Offener Großraum mit privaten Nischen

In einer Geriatrie vom flexiblen Menschen zu sprechen, wäre zynisch. Trotzdem steht auch hier dem Einzelnen das Recht zu, seine sozialen Beziehungen zu regulieren. In konventionellen geriatrischen Stationen mit Gängen und Zimmern ist für den Rückzug – bis zur totalen Vereinsamung – bestens gesorgt. Die Teilnahme an einem öffentlichen Leben beschränkt sich jedoch auf den Tagraum, wo sich die Gespräche in der Regel um die Frage drehen, auf welches Programm der dort aufgestellte Fernseher geschaltet werden soll. Schweighofer wollte dieses Prinzip auf den Kopf stellen. Seine Idealvorstellung für eine geriatrische Station ist der offene Großraum mit privaten Nischen, die im Normalfall offen stehen und nur bei Bedarf geschlossen werden. Selbst bettlägerige Bewohner sollten die Möglichkeit haben, vom Bett aus über eine elektrische Steuerung die Wände zur Gemeinschaftszone zu öffnen.

Geblieben ist von diesem Konzept eine breite, durch Einbauten gegliederte Innenzone mit vielfältigen Nutzungsmöglichkeiten. Die Räume zu beiden Seiten haben zwar keine Glaswände, aber zumindest große, zur Mittelzone hin orientierte Fenster mit Fensterläden aus Holz, die von innen gesteuert werden können. An der Stirnseite endet die innere Straße an einem großen Panoramafenster, das in den oberen Geschoßen einen prachtvollen Blick über Wien bietet. Die meisten Zimmer verfügen über kleine Wintergärten, deren Türen auf einen Balkon aufgehen und damit im Sommer einen erweiterten Freiraum bilden.

Large Open Space with Private Niches

To speak of flexible human beings in a geriatric care centre would be cynical. Nevertheless here too the individual has the right to determine his or her own social contacts. In conventional geriatric wards with corridors and rooms there is generally enough space to withdraw to – to the point of total isolation. Participation in public life is usually restricted to a dayroom where the conversation generally revolves around what television programme should be switched on. Schweighofer wanted to reverse this concept. His ideal image of a geriatric ward is the large open space with private niches that in the normal case are open and are closed only when required. Even bedridden residents should have the possibility to open the walls to the communal zone by means of an electronic control close to the bed. What survived of this concept is a broad inner zone, articulated by inserted elements, which can be used in different ways. While the rooms at either side do not have glass walls they have at least large windows oriented towards the centre zone with wooden shutters that can be operated from inside. The short ends of the inner street have a large panorama window that, on the upper floors, offers a marvellous view over Vienna. Most of the rooms have small winter gardens whose doors give onto a balcony and thus provide an expanded outdoor space in summer. Between two wards there is a shared service unit with treatment rooms for intensive care and service rooms for the staff.

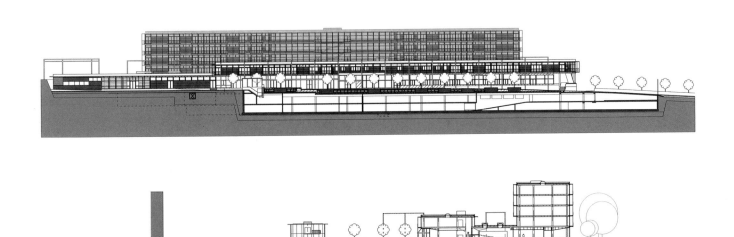

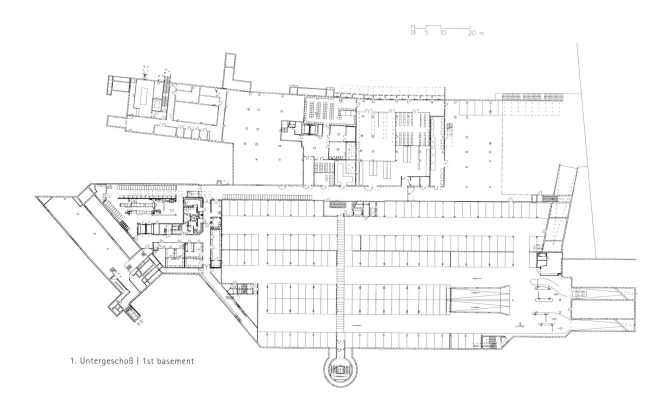

1. Untergeschoß | 1st basement

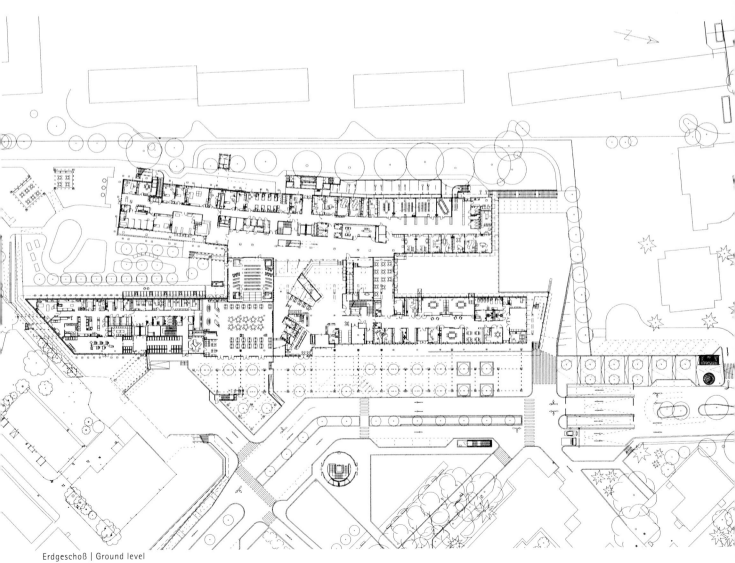

Erdgeschoß | Ground level

Zwischen den beiden Stationen befindet sich eine gemeinsame Serviceeinheit mit Behandlungsräumen für die Intensivpflege und Nebenräumen für das Personal. Hier liegt auch die Haupterschließung mit Liftkern und einer Treppe, die an der Glasfassade entlang führt. Jedes Geschoß erhält so ein großzügiges Foyer mit einer Art Wintergarten, das eine eigene Abstufung in der Hierarchie von privaten zu immer öffentlicheren Zonen bildet, die sich in der Eingangshalle mit Bistro und Lounge fortsetzt und schließlich vor dem Gebäude im Freien endet.

Antwort mit Vorbildwirkung

Schweighofer hat auf die Organisation der Freiräume besonderes Augenmerk gelegt. Er akzentuiert die neue Hauptzufahrt in das Krankenhaus mit einer begrünten, den niedrigen Baukörper überspannenden Pergola aus verzinktem Stahl, die von einer über der Tiefgarage gepflanzten Baumreihe begleitet wird. Zusätzlich zu diesen eher öffentlichen Freiflächen findet sich südseitig ein Gartenhof mit einer Freitreppe auf eine zwischen den beiden Hauptbaukörpern gelegene Terrasse, die von den Bewohnern fürs Gärtnern genutzt wird.

Here is where the main circulation is positioned with the lift core and a staircase that climbs along the glass façade. Each floor has a generous foyer with a kind of winter garden that represents a level of its own in the hierarchy from private to increasingly public zones that is continued in the entrance hall with the bistro and lounge and finally ends outside in front of the building.

A Response with Model Character

Schweighofer has devoted particular attention to the organisation of the open spaces. He accentuated the new main approach to the hospital with a plant-carrying pergola made of galvanised steel spanning the low building element and flanked by a row of trees planted above the underground garage. In addition to these more public outdoor spaces, on the south side there is a garden courtyard with a flight of steps to a terrace lying between the two main building elements that is used by the residents for gardening.

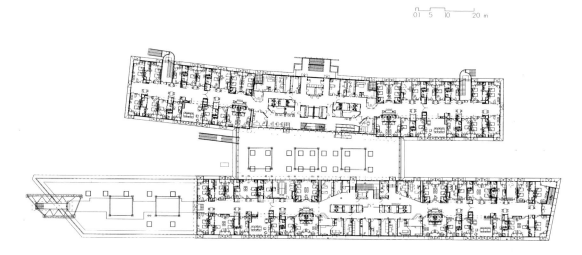

01 5   10   20 m

1. Obergeschoß | 1st level

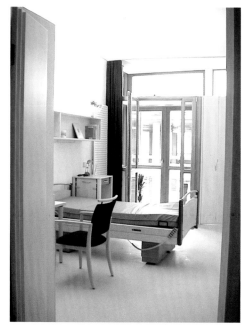

Individuelle Balkone und Kommunikationsraum
Private balconies and community space

Schweighofer hat mit diesem Projekt in konzeptioneller Hinsicht eine Summe seiner Architekturauffassung gezogen. Seine beiden Leitmetaphern sind das Haus als Stadt und das Haus als Baum: Einerseits horizontale Verflechtung von Wegen und Plätzen, andererseits vertikale Abfolge von Ästen und Blättern mit vielfältigen Blickbeziehungen bei der Bewegung von unten nach oben und umgekehrt. Das Projekt ist zugleich eine Summe von formalen Themen, die aus früheren Projekten vertraut sind: das Misstrauen gegenüber der zu exakten Lösung; die Überlagerung scheinbar gegensätzlicher Ideen, etwa der Auflösung der Fassade in ein lineares Geflecht aus Gitterstäben, die dann aber doch einen symmetrischen, beinahe klassisch organisierten Baukörper umspielen. Man merkt dem Bau an, dass Kompromisse geschlossen werden mussten, um diese Themen überhaupt neben funktionellen und finanziellen Parametern behandeln zu können. Bei einem Projekt dieser Komplexität und Dimension – bei dem Schweighofer zusammen mit seinem leitenden Mitarbeiter Peter Weber auch als Generalplaner aufgetreten ist – kann es im Detail aber nicht um Vollkommenheit gehen. Auf die Frage nach einem würdevollen Umfeld für die Pflege alter Menschen bietet dieses Haus jedenfalls eine Antwort, die Vorbildwirkung haben sollte.

In a conceptual sense Schweighofer has delivered in this project a summary of his understanding of architecture. His two guiding metaphors are the house as city and the house as a tree: on the one hand the horizontal linking of routes and squares, on the other the vertical sequence of branches and leaves with changing views and visual relationships during the movement up and down. This project is, so to speak, a summary of formal themes familiar from earlier projects: a distrust of excessively precise solutions; the overlaying of apparently contradictory or opposing ideas, such as the dissolution of the façade into a linear mesh of lattice rods that ultimately surround a symmetrical, almost classically organised building. One sees in this building that compromises had to made in order to deal with these themes within the strict functional and financial parameters. In a project of such complexity and size – where Schweighofer together with his leading staff member Peter Weber was also general planner – one cannot expect absolute perfection in the details. But in the question of how to provide dignified surroundings for the care of elderly people this building offers an answer that ought to serve as a model for the future.

**Geriatriezentrum Favoriten,
Küche & Garage SMZ-Süd**
Wien-Favoriten, Kundratstraße 3

Bauherr I client **KAV Krankenanstaltenverbund; MID GaragenerrichtungsgesmbH, Wien**
Planung I planning **Anton Schweighofer**
Projektleitung I project manager **Dipl. Ing. Peter Weber**
Mitarbeiter I assistance **Robert Kraska, Elisabeth Kreutzer, Stefan Thurnher, Claudia Oberwallner,
    Hannes Metzger, Brigitte Keller, Oliver Österreicher, Sergej Nikoljski**
Statik I structural consultant **Stella & Stengel & Partner, Wien**
Fassaden I facade **consultplan GmbH, Stoob; Rudolf Metallbau KG, Wien**
Brandschutztüren I fire doors **Tortec GmbH, Wien**
Haustechnik I mechanical services **Allplan, Wien**
Elektroinstallationen I electrical services **Landsteiner, Amstetten**
Sanitäre Installationen I plumbing **HTG, Wien; Insta Bloc, Wien**
Heizung/Lüftung/Klima I heating/ventilation/air conditioning **BACON Gebäudetechnik GmbH, Wien**
Küchenausstattung/Edelstahl I kitchen equipment/stainless steel **ACO Passavant, Baden**
Möbel I furnishings **Wiesner-Hager, Wien; HALI, Wien**
Lichtplanung I lighting concept **Trilux-Leuchten GesmbH, Wien**

Grundstücksfläche I site area	22.000 m²
Nutzfläche I floor area	
Geriatriezentrum	17.000 m²
Küche I kitchen	2.500 m²
Garage	11.300 m²
Bebaute Fläche I built-up area	7.200 m²
Umbauter Raum I cubage	
Geriatriezentrum	77.000 m³
Küche I kitchen	13.400 m³
Garage	41.700 m³
Planungsbeginn I start of planning	1996
Baubeginn I start of construction	1999
Fertigstellung I completion	2003
Baukosten I building costs	
Geriatriezentrum	32,7 Mio EUR
Küche I kitchen	7,6 Mio EUR
Garage	4,7 Mio EUR

Martin Kohlbauer

Volksschule und Kindertagesheim in Wien-Leopoldstadt
Elementary School and Children's Day Care Centre in Vienna-Leopoldstadt

Photos Rupert Steiner
Text Elke Krasny

Schule ist Architektur

Schulen sind, ohne dies plakativ zu annoncieren, alltägliche Räume des Architekturerfahrens, des Raumerlernens. In einer höchst heterogenen Situation, wo Verkehrsader und Peripherie einander begegnen, liegt die Volksschule Vorgartenstraße als markantes Merkzeichen an der U-Bahn-Linie. Zwischen zweigleisig geführter Hochtrasse sowie Gemeindebauten auf der einen Seite und Trabrennverein, Bildhauerateliers der Akademie, den ehemaligen *Pavillons des Amateurs* der Wiener Weltausstellung sowie der Wiener Messe auf den anderen Seiten, setzt der homogene Baukörper einen klaren städtebaulichen Akzent.

School is Architecture

Without announcing the fact in a too blatant a fashion, schools are everyday buildings where architecture and space can be experienced. In a highly heterogeneous situation where traffic arteries meet the periphery, the Vorgartenstrasse elementary school is located as a striking symbol on a Metro line. This homogenous building places a distinctive accent between the two tracks of the elevated railway and local authority housing on one side and the "Trabrennverein" (trotting race course), sculptors' studios belonging to the Academy of Fine Arts, former *Pavillons des Amateurs* from the Vienna World Fair and the modern Vienna Trade Fair on the other.

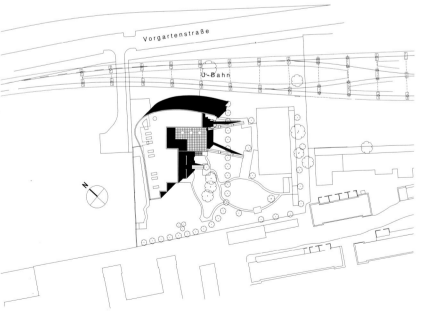

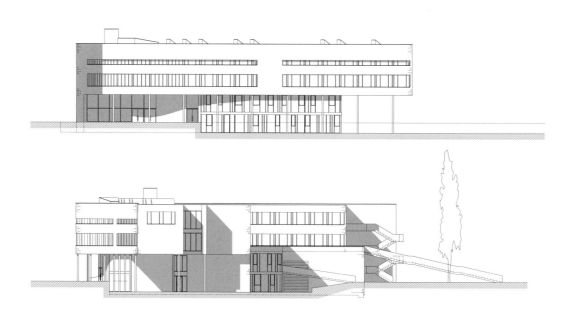

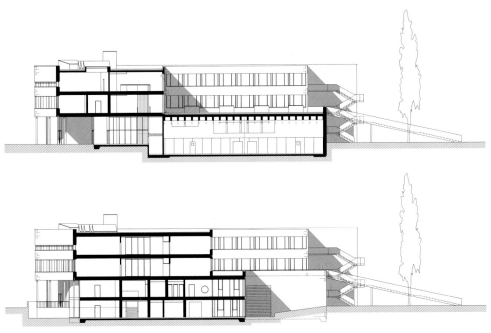

An der U-Bahn

Die Verlängerung der U-Bahn Linie U2 zu den Stadtbezirken
Leopoldstadt und Kagran sowie die Errichtung der dafür notwendigen neuen Trassen bedingten den Abriss der ehemals
hundert Meter vom jetzigen Standort befindlichen Vorgänger-
schule aus den 1960er Jahren. EU-weit wurde ein Bewerbungs-
verfahren ausgeschrieben, an dem sich hundert Architekturbüros für die Konzeption einer dreizehnklassigen Volksschule und
eines Kindertagesheims beteiligten. In der zweiten Runde des
Wettbewerbs mit geladenen Teilnehmern wurde der Entwurf
von Martin Kohlbauer als Siegerprojekt ausgezeichnet.
Gegen die in diesem Bereich als Hochbahn geführte U-Bahn-
Trasse (im Zweiminutentakt werden hier künftig die Züge vor-
beifahren) ist die Schule mit elegantem Schwung abgeschottet
und öffnet sich auf der anderen Seite großzügig und fließend
zum alten Baumbestand des Gartenareals. Von der U-Bahn aus
wird das öffentliche Gebäude als monolithische Skulptur, als
Wahrnehmungsruhepunkt aus seiner disparaten Umgebung
hervorstechen. Für die räumliche Organisation im Inneren bedeutete die Lage an der Verkehrsader und der beständig gegebene Lärm eine Herausforderung, Klassenräume wurden hier
nicht untergebracht. Der Bau zeigt der Trasse „die schöne, aber
kalte" Schulter und öffnet sich zur Gartenseite hin. Die Be-
tonsteinverkleidung mit zwei schmalen, von außen nicht ein-
sichtigen Fensterbändern, die von innen auf Kinderhöhe den
Blick auf U-Bahn und städtische Wohnhausanlagen freigeben,
unterstreicht den nach außen geschlossenen, gut geschützten
Eindruck. Der charakteristische Schwung und die Organisation

On the Metro Line

The construction of new tracks for the extension of the U2
Metro line to the suburban districts of Leopoldstadt and
Kagran required the demolition of the old school dating from
the 1960s, which stood around 100 metres from the site of the
new building. A competition open throughout the EU was set
up for a thirteen-classroom elementary school and children's
day care centre, and around one hundred architects' practices
submitted entries. In the second competition phase, (where
selected practices were invited to enter designs), Martin
Kohlbauer's scheme was chosen as the victorious project.
The school is screened by an elegant curve from the Metro
line, which here runs as an elevated railway at frequencies
of up to two minutes. On the other side the school opens
generously and flowingly towards the existing trees on the
garden-like site. Passengers on the trains will register the
public building as a monolithic sculpture, a point that offers
the perception a resting point in these highly disparate surroundings. The location on a traffic artery and the constant
noise represented a challenge for the internal organisation of
the building and it was decided not to locate the classrooms
on the side facing the Metro line. In fact the building shows
the railway line a "beautiful, but cold shoulder" and opens
towards the garden. The concrete block cladding and the two
narrow bands of glazing, which do not allow views from
outside into the building, but offer child-height views from
inside of the Metro and the urban housing developments, underline the impression of an externally closed, well-protected

in der L-Form entwickelte sich aus dem detaillierten Studium der Wirkungen des Orts. Der viergeschoßige, dennoch überraschend dezente, leicht anmutende Bau tritt in einen Dialog mit dem Baumbestand, zu dem er von innen heraus vielfache Blickbezüge und Zugangsmöglichkeiten entwickelt. Der im Osten des Gebäudes liegende Garten ist den in den beiden unteren Geschoßen untergebrachten Kindertagesheimgruppen direkt zugeordnet. Das Gelände wurde modelliert bis auf 1,7 Meter unter Niveau, ein halbes Geschoß weggenommen, um so die direkte Anbindung des Kindertagesheims an den Garten herzustellen. Gleichzeitig wurde durch die Geländemodellierung der Viergeschoßigkeit jegliche Massivität genommen.

Im Raumplan
Eine ungewöhnlich großzügige hallenartige Eingangssituation, welche die eineinhalbgeschoßige Raumhöhe auskostet, führt zu den um ein halbes Geschoß versetzten Ebenen von Hort und Kindertagesheim. Der Sportsaal liegt ein halbes Geschoß unter Eingangsniveau. Seine Stahlbetonrippendecke bildet zugleich die Terrasse für den Pausenhof. Entsprechende Gartenmöbel wurden von der Schulleitung sofort angekauft, und im Sommer gibt es hier sogar Freiluftunterricht. Die Terrasse ist einer der vielen Punkte, wo das durchgängige Entwurfskonzept der Verbindung zwischen Außen und Innen augenfällig wird. Möglichst nah wird das Außen, die Gartenanlage an und in das Innen herangeholt. Der ausgeklügelt verschlungenen, immer

building. The characteristic curve and the L-shaped organisation were developed out of a precise study of the character of the site. The four-storey yet surprisingly restrained and light building enters into a dialogue with the mature trees, establishing many visual links and approaches to them. The garden to the east of the building is directly allotted to the children's day care groups on the two lower floors of the building. The site was sculpted and excavated to a depth of 1.7 metres (half a storey) below the surrounding terrain to allow a direct connection between the day care centre and the garden. This modelling of the site also eliminates any sense of massiveness from the four-storey building.

In a "Raumplan"
An unusually generous hall-like entrance situation, which fully exploits its height of one and a half storeys, leads to the day care centre and after-school facilities that are staggered half a level. The gymnasium lies half a storey below the entrance level. The roof of the gymnasium is a ribbed reinforced concrete slab that provides a terrace used during school breaks. The school management soon purchased the appropriate garden furniture and in summer outdoor lessons can be held here. The terrace is one of the many points where the concept of connecting indoors and outdoors, which runs like a thread through the design, is particularly apparent. The outdoors and the garden are related as closely as possible to

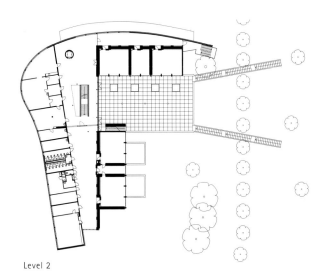

Level 2

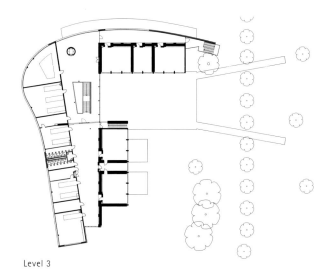

Level 3

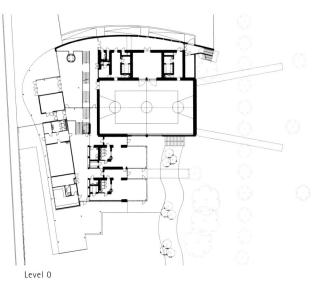

Level 0

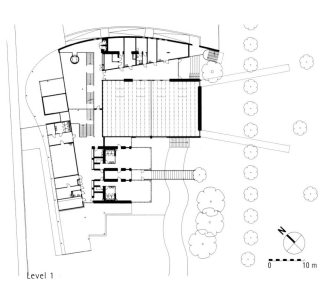

Level 1

Zentrale Halle | Main hall

wieder überraschenden und dennoch Halt und Orientierung im Raum bietenden inneren Organisation liegt die Idee eines Raumplanes im Split-Level-Prinzip zugrunde. Trotz des nach außen abgeschotteten Charakters wurde im Inneren größtmögliche Transparenz erreicht. Die zwei Gesichter der Schule nach außen, verschlossen zur U-Bahn, offen zum Garten, sind im Inneren nicht spürbar. Im Gegenteil, im Inneren wurde trotz Kompaktheit und homogener Geschlossenheit eine Durchsichtigkeit mit überraschend vielen Blickbezügen nach Außen erreicht, die nicht exponiert, sondern Licht und Grün ganz nah hereinholt.

the interior. The cleverly labyrinthine internal organisation that provides stability and orientation in space, while still full of surprises, is based on the idea of the "raumplan" and the split-level. Despite the externally aloof character the architect achieves a maximum of transparency inside the building. The two exterior faces of the building, closed to the Metro, open to the garden, are not noticeable in the interior. On the contrary, despite the compactness and the homogenous nature of the composition the architect achieves a transparency in the interior with surprising numbers of visual relationships to the outside, which do not expose the internal life of the school but yet bring light and greenery closer.

Eine einläufige kaskadenartige Treppe führt in die auf zwei Ebenen organisierten Klassenräume. Im Inneren des Schulhauses ist der dominierende Eindruck Weiß. Der klare Eindruck wird unterstrichen durch die bewusst gesetzte Lichtführung, das Hereinholen von Tageslicht an so vielen Stellen wie möglich und dem ausgetüftelten Kunstlichteinsatz, der ohnehin schon großzügig bemessene Verkehrsflächen wie Halle und Gänge noch weiter erscheinen lässt. Geschlossene silbrig-graue Garderobenschränke unterstreichen diesen Raumeindruck. Die orangen Kautschukböden sind physisch wie optisch wärmender Kontrast zum klaren Weiß und zum vom Garten hereingeholten Grün oder winterlich-herbstlichen Braun.

Fühler in den Hof

Nach außen wachsen aus der L-Form Fühler in den Hof. Der jetzige Bau wurde gegenüber dem Wettbewerb in reduzierter Form ausgeführt und ist so ausgerichtet, dass ein möglicher zweiter Bauabschnitt, der dann weitere Fühler in den Garten ausstrecken würde, im Falle des Bedarfs konstruktiv möglich wäre. Die beiden Brücken in den Hof, ausgebildet als Betonrampentreppen, strecken ihre Fühler in den Garten aus und bilden eine direkte Annäherung von Pausenterrasse zum Grünraum. Weite Gänge mit überraschenden Gartenblicken, Freiluftunterricht- oder Pausenterrasse, lange Rampen ins Grüne, all diese Räume tragen dem Bewegungs- und Raum-Erspürdrang von Kindern Rechnung. Aus dem Bezug zum alten Baumbestand und aus der deklarierten Außenorientierung resultieren Ein- und Ausschnitte für Räume und Funktionen im skulpturalen Baukörper, die die innenräumlichen Qualitäten steigern. Die zwei Gesichter des Baus sind stringent durchgehalten und komplex miteinander verschränkt, abgeschottet und zugleich offen, nicht exponierend und dennoch transparent, klar strukturiert und voll komplexer Überraschungen.

A cascading staircase leads to the classrooms that are organised on two levels. The dominant impression inside the school building is one of whiteness. The clear, white impression is underlined by the careful use of lighting, the introduction of daylight at as many points as possible and the clever use of light sources which makes circulation areas, such as the hall and the corridors that in any case are generously dimensioned, seem even more expansive. Closed silver grey lockers underline the dominant spatial impression. Orange rubber flooring provides a physically and visually warming contrast to the clear white of the walls and ceiling and to the green shades of summer or the brown tones of winter and autumn that are brought into the building from the garden.

Feelers in the courtyard

Feelers extend outwards from the L-shaped building into the courtyard. The present building is a reduced version of the successful competition project and is laid out in such a way that a possible second phase, which would extend further feelers into the garden, is structurally possible if required. The two bridges into the courtyard, which are made in the form of stepped concrete ramps, also stretch their feelers into the garden forming a direct connection from the terrace used during breaks to the green space. Further corridors with surprising views of the garden, open-air teaching areas, the terrace, long ramps extending into the greenery all represent spaces that cater to the children's need to move around and experience spaces. The relationship to the existing mature trees and the emphatically outward orientation create incisions and cutouts for different spaces and functions in the sculptural block of the building that intensify the spatial quality of the interior. While the concept of two distinct faces to the building is strictly adhered to, the two aspects are linked with each other in a complex way, closed off and yet open. Although the people and the life inside are never exposed, the building remains transparent, clearly structured and full of complex surprises.

Bibliothek und Sportsaal | Library and gymnasium

Volksschule & Kindertagesheim
Wien-Leopoldstadt, Vorgartenstraße 208

Bauherr I client **Stadt Wien, MA 56**
Planung I planning **Martin Kohlbauer**
Projektleitung I project manager **Hannes Venturo**
Statik I structural consultant **Vasko + Partner**
Fassaden/Mauerwerk I facade/masonry **Bilfinger & Berger, Wien**
Dach I roof **Ploberger, Wien**
Fenster I windows **Mandl + Eckl**
Türen I doors **Holzbau Weiz**
Elektroinstallationen I electrical services **Elektro Landsteiner, Amstetten**
Heizung/Lüftung/Klima/Sanitäre Installationen I heating/ventilation/air conditioning/
    plumbing **HTG, Wien**
Lichtplanung/-ausstattung I lighting concept/fittings **Knoblich; SITECO**
Böden I flooring **Zahalka, Wien**
Möbel I furnishings **Kaar, Bad Leonfelden**
Aufzug I elevators **Kogler, Pinkafeld**

Grundstücksfläche I site area	10.080 m²
Nutzfläche I floor area	4.735 m²
Bebaute Fläche I built-up area	1.905 m²
Umbauter Raum I cubage	23.544 m³
Planungsbeginn I start of planning	4/2001
Baubeginn I start of construction	4/2002
Fertigstellung I completion	7/2003
Baukosten I building costs	10,5 Mio EUR

BEHF

Wohnbau in Wien-Meidling
Apartment Block in Vienna-Meidling

Photos Rupert Steiner
Text Andrea Nussbaum

Ein Ziegelmonolith im Häusermeer

Der Wohnbau könnte in Berlin, Hamburg oder eben in Wien stehen. Auch sein Erbauungsjahr sieht man ihm nicht an. Diese ort- und zeitlose Sachlichkeit ist nicht nur von wohltuender visueller Qualität, sondern entspricht einer klaren planerischen Strategie.

A brick monolith in a sea of houses

This housing block could be in Berlin, Hamburg or Vienna. One cannot immediately say when it was built. This objectivity, divorced from a specific place or time, is not only a soothing visual quality, but also the result of a clear planning strategy.

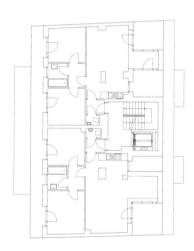

Dachgeschoß | Roof plan

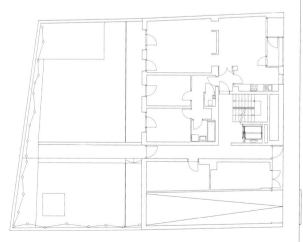

Erdgeschoß | Ground floor

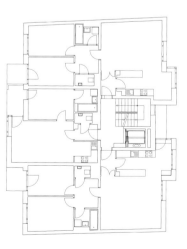

Regelgeschoß | Standard floor plan

Strenge Kiste mit Einschnitten | A severe box with incisions

Wohnungen für „junge, urbane Mieter"
Apartments for "young and urban tenants"

Architektur ohne Eigenschaften

Es sei eine strenge Kiste mit Einschnitten, so definiert Stephan Ferenczy von BEHF Architekten das Wohnhaus in Wien-Meidling. Ein dunkler Monolith, der sich in seiner Umgebung behauptet; einige hundert Meter außerhalb des Wiener Gürtels gelegen, in einem Stadtquartier, das vor allem eines ist: heterogen. Kleinbetriebe wie eine Autowerkstatt und ein Gebrauchtautohandel, daneben ragt ein riesiger Ziegelschornstein in die Höhe, eine kleinteilige gewerbliche Zone eben von Häusern unterschiedlichen Maßstabs umringt. Hier ist nichts, an dem man sich orientieren kann, hier herrscht jener „dirty realism" des „Beinahe"-Urbanen eines Wiener Außenbezirkes. Für eine „echte" Urbanität fehlt die atmosphärische Dichte, die Durchmischung, die Spannungen zwischen dem Gebauten. Und dennoch haben es BEHF geschafft, hier mit einem urbanen Wohnbau zu antworten. Ein Ziegel-Monolith, der sich nach außen verschließt, um sich nach Innen zu öffnen. Fünf Geschoße hat die dunkle „Hardware", wie BEHF gerne die harte Schale ihrer Bauten nennt. Der Hauseingang ist Innen an Wand und Boden ebenfalls noch in Ziegel ausgeführt, auch das Treppenhaus wirkt „rau" in Sichtbeton, die Wohnungstüren konsequent schwarz gestrichen. Umso erstaunlicher dann die Wohnungen, die zwar von ihren Größen – so der ausdrückliche Wunsch der Wohnbaugesellschaft – eher klein gehalten, dafür aber großzügig mit Balkonen und Terrassen ausgestattet sind. Freundlich, vor allem benutzerfreundlich. Ihr strahlendes Weiß steht im unmittelbaren Kontrast zur dunklen „Hardware". Man fühlt sich wie in einer anderen Welt.

Single, jung, urban

Der Markt verlangt nach kleineren Einheiten: 14 Wohnungen hat der Ziegelmonolith von BEHF, die erstmals nach ihren langjährigen Erfahrungen im Industrie-, Laden- und Kulturbau einen Geschoßwohnbau in Wien errichteten. Allen Apartments ist ein Freiraum in Form von Loggien zugedacht, den größeren in den oberen Geschoßen auch Terrassen. Und es zeugt von einem gewissen Luxus im geförderten Wohnbau, wenn man auch vom Badezimmer aus Zutritt auf den Balkon hat. Zum Wohnstandard gehören eine Tiefgarage mit 14 Stellplätzen (pro Wohnung eine), ein Außenbereich, der durch eine Ziegelwandscheibe zweigeteilt ist, in einen Mietergarten und einen Privatgarten, der zur ebenerdigen Wohnung gehört, die – nach dem holländischen Modell – mit eigenem Eingang von der Straße konzipiert ist. Jene ebenerdige Wohnung mit separatem Stra-

Architecture without qualities

A severe box with incisions, this is how Stephan Ferenczy from BEHF Architekten defines his new apartment house in Vienna-Meidling. A dark monolith that asserts itself in its surroundings: a few hundred metres outside Vienna's Gürtel ring road in a district that is one thing above all others: heterogeneous. Small businesses such as car repair workshops and used car premises, beside them a giant brick chimney soaring into the sky: a small-scale commercial zone surrounded by buildings of different scales. There is nothing to orient oneself on here, the "almost urban dirty realism" of Vienna's outer districts dominates. For a genuine urbanity there lacks any atmospheric density, the mixture, the tension between the different buildings. And yet BEHF have succeeded in providing an urban apartment building, a brick monolith that is outwardly closed but opens inwards. The dark "hardware", as BEHF like to term the hard shell of their buildings, has five storeys. In the entrance brick is used for the walls and floors, the staircase too seems somewhat "raw", as it is made of exposed concrete, and the entrance doors to the apartments are uniformly painted black. This makes the apartments all the more surprising: although in terms of size they are rather small (a requirement of the housing society client) they are generously equipped with balconies and terraces. Their gleaming white colour forms a direct contrast to the dark "hardware" and you feel as if you are in a different world.

Single, young, urban

The market calls for smaller units: BEHF's brick monolith contains 14 of them. After their many years of experience in industrial, shop and cultural buildings this is their first multistorey apartment building in Vienna. All of the apartments have an open space in the form of a loggia; the larger apartments on the upper floors also have terraces. And it indicates a certain degree of luxury in a subsidised housing project that one can walk from one's bathroom onto a balcony. Part of the housing standard is an underground garage with 14 parking spaces (one per apartment) an outdoor area that is divided by a brick wall into a tenants' garden and a private garden that belongs to the ground floor apartment, which, following Dutch examples, has its own entrance from the street. This ground floor apartment, with its separate entrance from the street and its own green space, is the largest and measures 100 square metres. The others range between 50 and

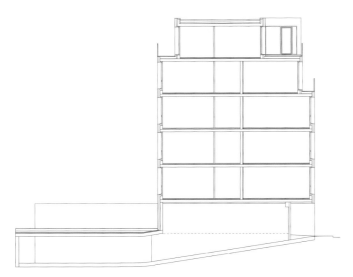

Schnitt | Section

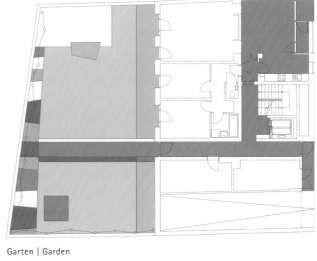

Garten | Garden

ßeneingang und eigenem Grünraum ist mit 100 m² die größte. Die anderen rangieren in Größen von 50 bis 85 m². Je höher die Geschoße, desto freizügiger die Grundrisse, und ganz oben zwei richtige kleine „Penthouses", die sich nach zwei Seiten hin entwickeln, mit kleinen und größeren Terrassen. „Man kann sich gut vorstellen, wie hier Menschen sitzen und Feste feiern." Genauso möchte Stephan Ferenczy seine Wohnungen sehen: urban kultiviert, individuell belebt. Wert gelegt hat BEHF bei allen, also auch bei den kleinsten Wohnungen von 50 m², auf eine klare Trennung zwischen Wohn- und Schlafzonen, also zwischen dem Gäste- und dem Privatbereich.

Ziegel ist Zukunft

Der bestechendste Eindruck ist allerdings jener der Ziegelfassade. Seine traditionelle, in Wien jedoch ungewöhnliche Referenz ist sachlich, solide, vor allem aber zeitlos. Jegliche Indizien für das Entstehungsjahr des Baus werden bewusst unterdrückt. Hier geht es um Wohnqualität und eine sich zurücknehmende Sprache, die dennoch ihre Kanten und Ecken hat, um sich zu behaupten. Der kraftvolle Ziegel, sein dunkles Manganbraun, die präzisen Einschnitte und die arhythmische Fensteranordnung, die konsequent den inneren Funktionen folgt, verleihen dem Bau Ausdruck, ohne aber aufdringlich zu wirken. Das Konzept der Zeitlosigkeit funktioniert, denn das „Modische", „Trendige" kommt mit den Mietern und geht auch wieder mit ihnen. Shops oder Restaurants sind für einen begrenzten Zeitrahmen geschaffen, beginnt man sich daran satt zu sehen, ändert man es, denn jeder neue Look zieht wieder neue Menschen an. Bei einem Wohnbau allerdings funktioniert das nicht: Ein Haus dieser Größe ist nicht nur aus wirtschaftlichen Gründen für länger konzipiert, hier beginnt sich die Idee der Zeitlosigkeit gestalterisch und visuell zu rechnen. Eine souveräne Qualität für einen spezifischen Ort in einem „beinahe"-urbanen Gefüge. Je länger man darüber nachdenkt, muss man sich fragen, warum solche Konzepte nicht viel öfter zu finden sind; Konzepte, die auch die Erhaltungsfragen miteinbeziehen, denn für eine Ziegelfassade fallen theoretisch in den nächsten 50 bis 100 Jahren keine Instandhaltungskosten an, an der Fassade muss nichts gemacht werden und sie wird trotzdem bleiben, wie sie ist. Vollständigkeitshalber sollte ein wichtiges, zeitgemäßes Detail nicht unerwähnt bleiben: Als Niedrigenergiehaus ist dieser Ziegelmonolith mit seinem zweischaligen Sichtziegelmauerwerk ganz sicher zukunftstauglich. Die gute Bauphysik und die hohe Speichermasse sorgen nicht nur für niedrige Energiekosten, sie schaffen auch ein gutes Raumklima.

85 square metres. The further up the building the more free the floor plans are, at the top two small "penthouses" open on two sides with smaller and larger terraces. "One can easily imagine people relaxing or holding parties here." This is exactly how Stephan Ferenczy wishes to view his apartments: urbane, cultivated and individually animated. BEHF laid emphasis on creating in all the units, even the smallest, 50-square-metre apartments, a clear separation between the living and sleeping areas, that is between the guest and private domains.

Brick is the future

The most abiding impression is that made by the brick façade. The traditional references are functionality, solidity and above all a certain timelessness. Any indications of the year in which the building was erected were deliberately suppressed. And in Vienna, brick façades are quite unusual. The issue here was domestic quality and a restrained formal language that in order to assert itself still has a certain edge to it. The powerful, dark manganese brown brickwork, the precise incisions and the non-rhythmical arrangement of the windows that consistently follows their function in the interior give the building an expression, without making it over imposing. The concept of timelessness has functioned, the trendy and fashionable elements comes with the tenants and leave with them again. Shops or restaurants are made for a limited lifespan, when people get tired of looking at them they are changed, as each new look attracts new customers. This approach does not work in an apartment building: a building of this size is, not just for economic reasons, designed for a longer lifespan, in such a situation the idea of timelessness begins to make sense, both visually and in design terms. This is a sovereign quality for a specific location in an "almost" urban mesh. The more one thinks about it, the more one is inclined to ask why such concepts are not more common, concepts that in their own way also deal with maintenance questions, for, over the next 50 to 100 years, the brick façade will theoretically require no maintenance, nothing must be done to the façade so that it remains the way it is. For the sake of completeness an important contemporary detail should not be left unmentioned. As a low-energy building this brick monolith with its two layers of fair-faced brickwork is certainly equipped for the future. The good building physics and the high-energy storage capacity not only ensure low energy costs; they also create a pleasant internal climate.

Ansicht vom Garten | View from the garden

Wohnbau
Wien-Meidling, Kollmayergasse 18

Bauherr | client **GPA Wohnbauvereinigung für Privatangestellte, Wien**
Generalunternehmer | building contractor **Universale Hochbau Wien**
Planung | planning **BEHF Architekten**
Projektverantwortlicher | project supervision **Stephan Ferenczy**
Projektleitung | project manager **Petra Schramm**
Mitarbeiter | assistance **Robert Mago, Markus Weber, Liz Zimmermann, Petra Fehringer**
Generalplaner/Statik | general planning/structural consultant **Fritsch Chiari & Partner Ziviltechniker GmbH**
Bauphysik | construction physics **Dr. Pfeiler GmbH**
Fassade | facade **Keller Ziegeleien AG**
Haustechnik/Planung | mechanical services planning **Euro-Tec**
Elektroplanung | electrical concept **P.H.I. Technisches Planungsbüro**
Visualisierung | visualisation **Florian Hirschmann, Wien**
Modell | model **F. Haas, Modellbau Strasser**

Grundstücksfläche	site area	432 m²
Nutzfläche	floor area	998 m²
Bebaute Fläche	built-up area	260 m²
Mietergarten	tenants' garden	104 m²
Gemeinschaftsfläche	common area	80 m²
Planungsbeginn	start of planning	8/2002
Baubeginn	start of construction	8/2003
Fertigstellung	completion	10/2004
Baukosten	building costs	1,4 Mio EUR

schluderarchitektur

Wohnbau in Wien-Simmering
Housing Development in Vienna-Simmering

Photos Roman Bönsch
Text Robert Temel

Wohnen und Integration

Migranten sind kein Randphänomen mehr: Etwa ein Viertel der Wiener Bevölkerung hat einen ausländischen Pass, ist in den vergangenen vier Jahrzehnten eingewandert oder ist hier geborenes Kind von Migranten. Und da Wohnungen heute über Themen und damit äußerst zielgruppenspezifisch verkauft werden, kann diese Tatsache auch am Wohnungsmarkt nicht ignoriert werden.

Housing and Integration

Migrants are no longer a peripheral phenomenon. Around one quarter of the population of Vienna has a foreign (i.e. non-Austrian) passport, has immigrated within the past four decades or was born here as to migrant parents. And, as these days apartments are marketed according to themes and are therefore closely related to specific target groups, this fact can no longer be ignored on the housing market.

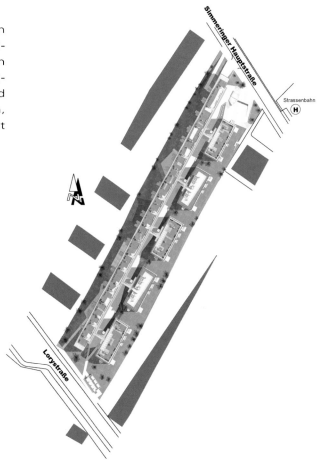

Raum für Kommunikation

Bereits bei Wohnbauten in der Donau-City, die Ende der 1990er Jahre fertig gestellt worden waren, galt das Verkaufsargument des kosmopolitischen Stadtteils mit internationalem Flair – auch, aber nicht nur durch die nahe liegende UNO-City bedingt. Bauträger, die nicht nur in Marketing denken, sondern auch politische Ideen verfolgen, – übrigens durchwegs gemeinnützige – deklarieren dem gegenüber Projekte offen als „integrativ". Bereits 1996 stellte die GEWOG mit den Architekten Heidecker & Neuhauser die Anlage „Interkulturelles Wohnen" in Florids- dorf fertig. 2000 folgte die „Interethnische Nachbarschaft" in Liesing, errichtet von der Sozialbau AG mit den Architekten Lautner-Scheifinger-Szedenik-Schindler, und nun realisierte die Wohnbauvereinigung für Privatangestellte (WBV-GPA) mit Architekt Schluder ein integratives Wohnprojekt an der Sim- meringer Hauptstraße.

All diesen Projekten ist gemeinsam, dass ihre Bewohnerschaft sich etwa zur Hälfte aus Österreichern und zur anderen aus Migranten zusammensetzt, dass also das gesellschaftspolitische Modell der Integration im Kleinen eingelöst werden soll, in- dem die Bewohner aus verschiedenen „kulturellen Kontexten" einander durch gemeinsames Wohnen kennen lernen und da- bei ethnische Segregation auflösen. Soziale Segregation kann durch einzelne Wohnbauten natürlich nicht reduziert werden,

Space for Communication

In the case of housing developments in the Donau-City that were completed at the end of the 1990s the sales argument was based on the notion of a cosmopolitan urban district with an international flair, influenced (but not exclusively) by the proximity of the UNO headquarters. Developers that do not think just in terms of marketing but also pursue political objectives – incidentally for the most part non-commercial developers – openly declare such projects to be integrative. As early as 1996 GEWOG completed the complex "Interculturelles Wohnen" ("Intercultural Living") designed by architectes Heidecker & Neuhauser in Floridsdorf. In 2000 there followed the "Interethnische Nachbarschaft" ("Inter-ethnic Neighbour- hood") in Liesing erected by Sozialbau AG and designed by architects Lautner-Scheifinger-Szedenik-Schindler, and now the Housing Association for Private Employees (WBV-GPA) with their architect Schluder are carrying out an integrative housing project on Simmeringer Hauptstrasse.

All these projects have in common the fact that about one half of their residents are Austrians and the other half is made up of migrants. The aim is to realise the socio-political model of integration at a small scale by enabling residents from dif- ferent "cultural contexts" to get to know each other through living together, thus putting an end to ethnic segregation. Of

dafür sind politische Maßnahmen wie die Gleichstellung am Wohnungsmarkt nötig. Da nun aber Wohnanlagen im kulturellen Kontext Wiens nicht gerade Kommunikationsmaschinen sind, ähneln die integrativen Projekte einander auch in anderer Hinsicht als der Zusammensetzung ihrer Bewohnerschaft: Sie alle basieren auf architektonischen Konzepten, die Begegnung und Gemeinschaft ermöglichen oder zumindest ausdrücken sollen. Das wirkt sich einerseits auf die Erschließungsflächen aus, die bei allen genannten Projekten aus Laubengängen bestehen, und andererseits auf ein relativ breites Angebot an Gemeinschaftsflächen wie Veranstaltungs- und Freiräumen zusätzlich zu den vorgeschriebenen Flächen. Man könnte interpretieren, dass man in Migranten aus vermeintlich kommunikativeren Kulturen die Hoffnung setzt, die Österreicher zu einem Modell des gemeinschaftlichen Wohnhauses zurückzuführen, das als heute verloren angesehen wird – dies scheint mit doch erheblichem räumlichen Aufwand forciert zu werden.

Transparente Erschließungen

Der Bauherr WBV-GPA entschied sich für einen Wohnbau mit dem Schwerpunkt Integration aufgrund der Erfahrungen mit dem 1999 für das Innenministerium errichteten Kardinal-König-Flüchtlingswohnheim in Simmering, aus dem die dort aufgenommenen Flüchtlinge nach fünf Jahren ausziehen müssen,

course it is impossible to completely overcome social segregation by individual housing projects alone, political measures, such as equality of opportunity on the housing market, are also necessary. As housing developments in the cultural context of Vienna are not exactly communication machines, the integrative projects tend to resemble each other in other aspects apart from the ethnic origins of their residents: they are all based on architectural concepts that allow, or are at least intended to express, encounter and community. This is shown, for example, in the circulation areas, which in all the projects mentioned above are based on a deck access system, and also by a relatively wide range of communal areas such as events spaces and outdoor areas that are additional to the areas stipulated by the building authorities. One could see this as a hope that migrants from supposedly more communicative cultures could eventually lead the Austrians back to a more communally-based understanding of housing, a notion today regarded by and large as lost – this concept seems to be promoted here with considerable expenditure in terms of space.

Transparent Circulation

The developer WBV-GPA decided to build a housing project that placed the emphasis on integration as a result of experience they had gained with the Cardinal König refugees hostel

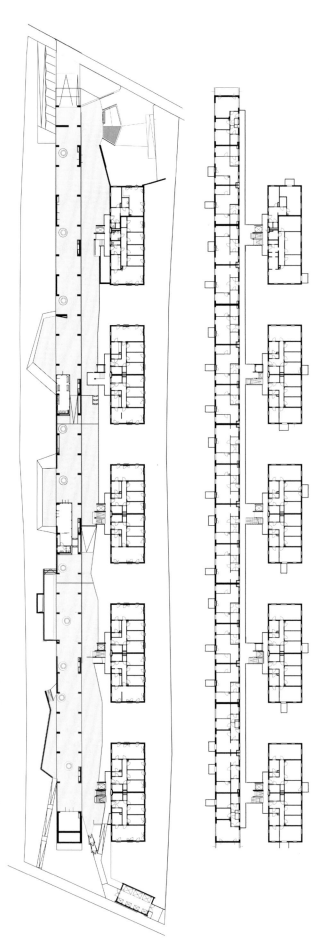

um sich am Wohnungsmarkt eine neue Bleibe zu suchen. Diese unfreiwillig Wohnungssuchenden waren die ersten Adressaten des neuen Projektes, etwa 15 Wohnungen wurden an ehemalige Heimbewohner vergeben. Diese Haltung ist dem Bauträger hoch anzurechnen.

Die architektonischen Qualitäten des Wohnbaus überzeugen auch unabhängig von der Ausrichtung als integratives Wohnprojekt: Das Gebäude wurde auf einem extrem lang gestreckten, schmalen Grundstück errichtet, das mit seiner Schmalseite zur Simmeringer Hauptstraße liegt. Links und rechts davon befindet sich eine Wohnbauanlage aus den späten 1960er Jahren, die aus orthogonal angeordneten, vier- und achtgeschoßigen

in Simmering, erected in 1999 for the Ministry of the Interior. After a maximum stay of five years the refugees accommodated there must leave the hostel and find new accommodation on the housing market. These people, who, through no fault of their own, are confronted with a search for accommodation, were the initial target of this new project and around 15 apartments were allotted to former hostel residents. Great respect is due to the developer for taking this approach.

Quite apart from its function as an integrative housing project the architectural qualities of the development are convincing. The building was erected on an extremely elongated, narrow site with a short end facing onto Simmeringer Hauptstrasse.

Zeilen mit großzügigen Grünflächen dazwischen besteht. Der Neubau ordnet sich einerseits mit seiner langen Zeile von fast 200 Metern in diesen Raster ein und schließt die vorhandenen grünen Höfe, hält aber gleichzeitig die visuelle Durchlässigkeit aufrecht, weil er etwa vier Meter aufgeständert ist und somit im Erdgeschoß keine Barriere bildet. Die Erschließungsflächen, Stiegen und Laubengänge, sind durchwegs offen, und das freie Erdgeschoß dient als überdeckter, halböffentlicher Platz, der durch gläserne Raumboxen für Waschküche und Kindergruppen gegliedert wird. Leider ist die Transparenz aber nur visuell, da Zäune an der Grundstücksgrenze und zwischen den Mietergärten den Durchgang versperren.

To the left and right of the site is housing development dating from the late 1960s that consists of four and eight-storey blocks laid out on rectilinear pattern with large areas of green space between them. The new development, with a block almost 200 metres long, fits into this grid and terminates the existing green courtyards, while at the same time preserving visual permeability, as it is raised on piers four metres above ground level and therefore does not form a barrier at ground floor level. The circulation spaces, staircases and access decks are completely open, and the free ground floor area serves as a sheltered semi-public space that is articulate by glazed boxes that house the laundry and offer space for various

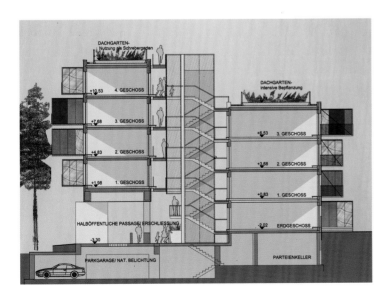

Reiz der Vielfalt

Die lang gestreckte Nordseite der Zeile in schwarzem Eternit ist durch großzügige, mit bunten Windschutzsegeln versehene Balkons gegliedert, die auf dieser Fassade das Bild einer Vielzahl von Nationalflaggen erzeugen, auch wenn keine der Farbkombinationen eine Entsprechung in der Realität hat. Südöstlich sind der Zeile fünf gelb verputzte, halbgeschoßig versetzte Punkthäuser vorgelagert, die durch die Stiegenhäuser mit der Zeile verbunden sind. Im Raum zwischen der Zeile und der Punkthausreihe, gegliedert durch die offenen Stiegenhäuser und Lifttürme, entsteht so eine Abfolge von in Längsrichtung visuell geschlossenen, halböffentlichen Außenräumen, die sich quer unter der Zeile hindurch und zwischen den Punkthäusern zu den Höfen der Nachbaranlage öffnen. Die Punkthäuser enthalten große, vorrangig südorientierte Wohnungen mit vier bis fünf Zimmern, während in der Zeile Wohnungen mit zwei bis drei Zimmern untergebracht sind. In der Zeile beträgt die lichte Breite nur sechs Meter, sodass in den kleinen Wohnungen eine helle, luftige Atmosphäre entsteht. Auf den Dächern befinden sich Gemeinschaftsterrassen und Mietergärten. Darüber hinausgehend bietet die Anlage einen großzügigen Veranstaltungsraum mit Küche und Öffnung zu einem Freiplatz, einen Proberaum sowie eine Boulebahn für die Bewohner. Und das offene Erdgeschoß ist so groß, dass es als Potenzial für zukünftige, einfach zu bewerkstelligende Raumergänzungen verstanden werden kann. Das integrative Wohnprojekt bietet außerhalb der privaten Räume eine für geförderten Wohnbau erstaunliche Vielfalt an nutzbaren Innen- und Außenräumen, die man sich für jedes Projekt wünschen würde – und es nimmt Bezug auf die vorhandenen, aber selten gewürdigten Qualitäten des Wohnbaus der 1950er und 1960er Jahre, die hier durch den Neubau eine adäquate Ergänzung erfahren.

children's groups. Unfortunately, this transparency is only visual, as fences along the site boundary and between the tenants' gardens block the way through.

The Attraction of Diversity

The elongated north side of the block is clad in black fibre cement and is articulated by generously dimensioned balconies with colourful wind protection sails that make the facade look like a collection of different flags, even though none of the colour combinations represents a real national flag. To the south-east of the block are five yellow rendered point buildings, staggered half a level, which are connected to the main block by staircases. The space between the long block and the point buildings is articulated by the open staircase elements and lifts towers, creating a sequence of visually defined, semi-public outdoor spaces on the long axis that continues under the long block and between the point buildings to the courtyards of the neighbouring complex. The point buildings contain large, primarily south-facing apartments, whereas the long block has two- and three-room apartments. The long block is only six metres deep so that the small apartments have a bright and airy atmosphere. On the roof there are communal terraces and tenants' gardens. In addition the complex boasts a sizable events room that opens to an outdoor area and is equipped with a kitchen, a rehearsals room as well as a boules alley for the residents. The open ground floor is so large that it can be viewed as potential for future spatial additions that would be easy to make. In addition to the private spaces this integrative housing projects offers a range of usable indoor and outdoor spaces most unusual in subsidised housing, something one might wish for in every project of this kind – and it takes up the existing but rarely praised qualities of the housing from the 1950s and 1960s and appropriately augments and enhances them.

Wohnanlage
Wien-Simmering, Simmeringer Hauptstraße 192a

Bauherr | client **Wohnbauvereinigung für Privatangestellte, Wien**
Generalunternehmer | building contractor **ÖSTU-STETTIN Hoch- & Tiefbau GmbH, Leoben**
Planung | planning **schluderarchitektur**
Entwurf | design **Schluder/Kastner**
Mitarbeiter | assistance **Natascha Stoklaska**
Projektleitung | project manager **Dipl. Ing. Martin Leopold, Leopold+Wallack OEG, Graz**
Statik | structural consultant **Zemler + Raunicher ZT GmbH, Wien**
Fassaden | facade **Bauer Fassaden GmbH, Wien**
Dach | roof **Carl Günther GesmbH, Wien; steinodus UKD/Steinbacher Dämmstoff GmbH, Erpfendorf**
Mauerwerk | masonry **Wienerberger AG, Wien**
Fenster | windows **Hrachowina GmbH, Wien**
Türen | doors **Katzbauer GmbH, Graz**
Elektroinstallationen | electrical services expert **Babinsky, Hollabrunn**
Heizung/Lüftung/Klima/Sanitäre Installationen | heating/ventilation/air conditioning/plumbing
    Ing. Georg Wieselthaler GesmbH, Schwechat
Aufzug | elevators **ThyssenKrupp Aufzüge, Wien**

Grundstücksfläche	site area	7.845 m²
Nutzfläche	floor area	11.132 m²
Bebaute Fläche	built-up area	2.350 m²
Umbauter Raum	cubage	27.730 m³
Tiefgarage	basement garage	7.290 m³
Planungsbeginn	start of planning	10/2001
Baubeginn	start of construction	2/2003
Fertigstellung	completion	11/2004
Baukosten	building costs	9,3 Mio EUR
Kosten pro m²	cost per m²	835,– EUR

Johannes Will

„City Lounge", Wohngestaltung in Wien-Landstraße
"City Lounge", apartment design in Vienna-Landstraße

Photos Paul Ott
Text Elke Krasny

Fließend präzise

Reduziert man Wohnen auf seine notwendigen Funktionen, so schafft man Platz für die Wirkung des Raums durch sich selbst, für die Entfaltung von Licht und Schatten. Das Ideal der Leere, Konzentration auf einfache, prägnante Elemente und fließende Raumübergänge kennzeichnen die 150 m² große Altbauwohnung, die durch Mauerdurchbrüche ein neues Raumgefüge erhielt. Gerade in der Reduktion der Elemente, in der betonten Zurücknahme des Gestalterischen, entfalten die gesetzten Eingriffe ihre Kraft. Hervorstechendste Maßnahme war die Fragmentierung der Hauptmauer. So entstanden zwischen dem Bad-Küchen-Bereich und der Wohnzone türlose Durchgänge. Die Hauptachse der Wohnung wird betont und der Großflächigkeit der verwendeten Materialien ein skulpturaler, dreidimensionaler Kontrapunkt entgegengesetzt.

A Flowing Precision

By reducing living to its essential functions one can create room for the effects made by the space itself, for the play of light and shadows. The ideal of emptiness and concentration on basic striking elements and flowing spatial transitions are the characteristics of the 150-square-metre apartment in an old building, that was given a new spatial system by the removal of walls and openings. It is precisely the reduction in the number of elements and the emphasised restraint in the design interventions that helps them develop their particular effectiveness. The most striking measure was the fragmentation of the main wall to create doorways without doors between the bathroom-kitchen area and the living zone. The main axis of the apartment is emphasized and a sculptural, three-dimensional counterpoint made to the large areas of materials.

Schräge Formen

Die schräge, eingeschnittene Form der fragmentierten Wand, deren eine Öffnung verglast wurde, wird in den Regalen wieder aufgenommen. Der große Raum wird durch ein Regal als transparenter Raumteiler in Wohn- und Arbeitsbereich strukturiert. Bei Abendbeleuchtung verschwinden die gläsernen Teile des Regals, der schwebende Charakter kommt zum Vorschein. Zwischen dem transparenten Bad, das ganz ohne Fliesen auskommt, Harzplatten aus dem Schiffbau wurden hier verwendet, und dem Küchenblock bildet ein großer Abstand eine kommunikative Zone. Nicht nur die Räume entfalten hier ihre Kommunikation miteinander, ganz wörtlich kann sich hier menschliche Kommunikation zwischen Gästen entwickeln.

Alle Küchengeräte, Waschmaschine, Geschirrspüler und ähnliches ist hinter Schiebeelementen verborgen. Der fließende, ungestörte Raumeindruck wird durch die durchgehende Vermeidung von Fugen oder Türen und Klinken unterstrichen. Die privaten Bereiche, Schlafen, Garderobe fürs Umziehen, sind vom Wohnbereich abgeschottet. Man erreicht sie vom Vorzimmer durch ein raumhohes Eichenschiebeelement. Ein blickdichter Vorhang, wie er in der Bühnentechnik verwendet wird, schützt den Schlafraum gegen Licht und Einblicke. Alle verwendeten Materialien, Glas, Glasfolie, Nussparkett für den Boden, Eiche für Verkleidungen respektive Schiebeelemente kommen in unverfälschter Erscheinung zum Einsatz. Die Präzision des Entwurfs resultiert aus einem präzisen Raumstudium vor Ort, das vor allem auch die verschiedenen Lichtsituationen zu unterschiedlichen Tageszeiten in die Konzeption einbezog. Reduktion auf das Wesentliche bedeutet, den Raum, Licht, Schatten, Material in ihrer Eigensprachlichkeit zu Wort kommen zu lassen und so distinkte, vor allem großzügige Raumqualitäten zu schaffen.

Angled forms

The angled and incised form of the fragmented wall, one of whose openings is glazed, is taken up again by the shelving. A shelf, which functions as a transparent space divider in the living and working areas, structures the large space. When the light is switched on in the evening the glazed elements of the shelf tend to vanish and its hovering character becomes predominant. The considerable distance between the transparent bathroom that has no tiling at all (resin panels employed in shipbuilding were used instead) and the kitchen block forms a communication zone. Not only do the spaces communicate with each other, human communication between guests can also develop.

All kitchen appliances, washing machine, dishwasher etc., are concealed behind sliding elements. The flowing undisturbed spatial impression is underlined by the consistent avoidance of joints or doors and door handles. The private areas (sleeping area, dressing room) are screened off from the living area. They are reached from the hall through a full-height sliding element. An opaque drop, much like a stage curtain, protects the bedroom from light and enquiring gazes. All the materials employed (glass, glass and foil, nut parquet flooring, oak for the wood cladding of the sliding elements) are used in an honest way. The precision of the design results from a precise study of the space made on site that included above all the various lighting situations during the different times of the day. Reduction to essentials means allowing space, light shadows and materials to use their own language and thus to create distinct and, above all, excellent spatial qualities.

Wohnungsumbau
Wien-Landstraße, Fasangasse 49

Planung I planning **Johannes Will**
Projektleitung I project manager **Johannes Will**
Statik I structural consultant **Dipl. Ing. Pfeil, Wien**
Tischlerarbeiten/Türen/Wandverkleidungen I carpentry/doors/panelling
      WILLL Manufaktur, Großglobnitz
Baumeister I master builder **Leyrer+Graf, Wien**
Elektroinstallationen I electrical services **Rauch, Kirchberg**
Böden I flooring **Wallner, Groß Gerungs**
Heizung/Lüftung/Klima/Sanitäre Installationen I heating/ventilation/air conditioning/plumbing
      Krenn, Waidhofen/Thaya
Möbel I furnishings **WILLL Moebelkultur, Großglobnitz**

Nutzfläche I floor area	150 m²
Planungsbeginn I start of planning	1/2004
Baubeginn I start of construction	4/2004
Fertigstellung I completion	8/2004

Luigi Blau

Wohnungsumbau in Wien-Innere Stadt
Apartment conversion in Vienna's Inner City

Photos Margherita Spiluttini
Text Matthias Boeckl

Wiener Wohnkultur

Wien ist eine kultivierte Stadt. Und Wien verfügt auch über Architekten, die diese Kultur
und ihre Geschichte zum Sprechen bringen können. Luigi Blau zeigt mit seinen subtilen
Interieurs, dass die Lehren der historischen Moderne keineswegs vergessen sind. Und
dass es so etwas gibt wie einen modernen, bürgerlichen Lebensstil. Am besten lässt
sich das in der Innenstadt demonstrieren, die sich ihrer alten Funktion als pied-à-terre für
Wohlhabende mit mehreren weiteren Wohnsitzen immer weiter annähert.

Viennese Domestic Design

Vienna is a cultivated city. And Vienna also has architects that can give this culture
and its history a voice. In his subtle interiors Luigi Blau shows that the lessons of
historic modernism are far from being forgotten, and that there exists such a thing
as a modern, upper middle-class life style. This is best demonstrated in the inner city,
which is increasingly approaching its old function as a pied-à-terre for well-off people
with several other residences.

Kochbereich mit Frühstücksnische und Essplatz | Kitchen with breakfast alcove and dining place

Erweiterte Öffnung zum Wohnbereich
Enlarged passage to living area

Der „Alterssitz" für eine Amerikanerin und einen Schweizer, die in den wichtigsten Hauptstädten der Welt gearbeitet haben, ist mit 250 Quadratmetern großzügig bemessen und auch lagemäßig nahe dem Stephansdom bevorzugt. Ein solides Gründerzeithaus, das die gewohnt flexible Struktur mit großen, straßenseitigen Zimmern und rückseitiger Gangerschließung bot, wurde an heutige Bedürfnisse durch mehrere Eingriffe angepasst. Einige Wände wurden zwecks Herstellung größerer Raumeinheiten entfernt und die Öffnung einer tragenden Wand vergrößert, um einen angemessenen Wohn-, Koch- und Speiseraum zu ermöglichen. Alles hier ist gediegen, das Meiste in Maßarbeit angefertigt und nur die edelsten Materialien wie Marmor, Nuss- und Kirschholz verwendet. Neben dem multifunktionalen Salon mit Kamin, Frühstückserker sowie Koch- und Essbereich gibt es auch noch Arbeits- und Gästezimmer, Schlafzimmer und großzügige Sanitärbereiche. Die einzelnen historischen Möbel sind im Sinne Josef Franks kunterbunt gemischt, was durch die hohe Qualität jedes einzelnen legitimiert ist. Gerne bezieht sich Luigi Blau auf diese Wohnkultur der klassischen Moderne Österreichs. Hier zitiert er etwa Oskar Strnad, der glaubte, „dass Möbel und Wohnung weniger eine künstlerische Angelegenheit als vielmehr eine Sache des ‚kulturellen Anstandes' sind". Diese kulturelle Orientierung bringt Blau selbst auf den Punkt: „Ich versuchte, einer kosmopolitischen Familie in der Tradition der ‚Wiener Wohnkultur' – heute eher ein architekturhistorischer Begriff – eine WOHNUNG einzurichten."

The home for the "old age" of an American woman and a Swiss man who have worked in the most important world capitals, is generously dimensioned with a floor area of 250 square metres and enjoys an ideal location close to St Stephen's Cathedral. A solid, late 19th century building that offered the usual flexible structure with large rooms on the street front and an access corridor at the rear was adapted to meet contemporary requirements by several interventions. A number of walls were removed to make larger spaces and an opening in a load-bearing wall was increased in size to allow an appropriate living, cooking and dining space. Everything here is quietly elegant and mostly made to measure, using only the finest materials such as marble, nut and cherry wood. In addition to the multi-functional salon with fireplace, breakfast bay window and cooking and eating areas there are also guest rooms and working areas, bedrooms and spacious bathrooms. The individual pieces of old furniture are mixed and matched much in the manner of Josef Frank, which is perfectly legitimate, given the high quality of each individual piece. Luigi Blau likes to refer to the domestic design of classic Austrian modernism. He here quotes Oskar Strnad who believed that "furniture and an apartment are less an artistic matter rather than a question of 'cultural integrity'". Blau himself defines this cultural orientation as follows: "Following the tradition of 'Viennese domestic design' – which today is more an architectural historical concept – I attempted to make a HOME for a cosmopolitan family."

Bestand / Umbau | Former structure / Conversion

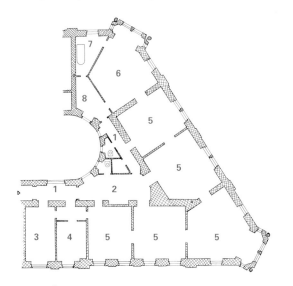

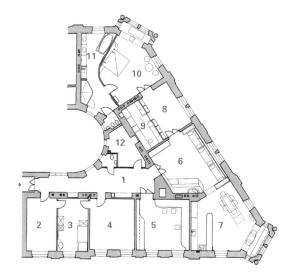

1 Gang / Hallway
2 Vorzimmer | Antechamber
3 Küche | Kitchen
4 Diener | Maid
5 Zimmer | Room
6 Schlafzimmer | Bedroom
7 Bad | Bath
8 Garderobe | Wardrobe

1 Vorzimmer / Antechamber
2 Gast | Guest
3 Bad und Wirtschaftsraum | Bath & chamber
4 Arbeitszimmer | Office
5 Arbeitszimmer | Office
6 Wohnen | Living room
7 Kochen und Essen | Kitchen & Dining
8 Bibliothek | Library
9 Garderobe | Wardrobe
10 Schlafzimmer | Bedroom
11 Bad | Bath
12 Abstell- und Technikraum | Storage & mechanical services

Maßmöbel und Kunst-Klassiker
Made to measure furniture and art classics

Wohnungsumbau
Wien, Innere Stadt

Bauherr I client **Familie P. & M. M.**
Planung I planning **Luigi Blau**
Mitarbeiter I assistance **My Tien Nguyen**
Statik I structural consultant **Prof. Dr. Dipl. Ing. Karlheinz Wagner**
Mauerwerk I masonry **Bauunternehmen Hammerl**
Haustechnik/Planung I mechanical services planning **Global Engineering**
Elektroinstallationen I electrical services **Elektrotechnik Gruner**
Heizung/Lüftung/Klima/Sanitäre Installationen I
heating/ventilation/air conditioning/plumbing **Freytag**
Bödenl flooring **Hochholdinger**
Möbel I furnishings **Schwarzott**
Maler/Anstrich I painting **F. Macke GesmbH**
Metallarbeiten I metalwork **Ludwig Kyral**

Wohnungsgröße I apartment	260 m²
Planungsbeginn I start of planning	11/2003
Baubeginn I start of construction	2/2004
Fertigstellung I completion	6/2004

Falkeis & Falkeis-Senn

Dachausbau der Universität für angewandte Kunst, Wien
Attic Conversion in the University of Applied Arts, Vienna

Photos Pez Hejduk
Text Matthias Boeckl

Luft-Räume

Dachausbauten sind eine wesentliche Ressource des Stadtumbaus und gerade Wien verfügt hier mit seinem großen Bestand gründerzeitlicher Bauten über umfangreiche, besterschlossene Raumreserven. Im beharrlichen Tauziehen zwischen Denkmalschutz und sinnvollen Umnutzungsplänen entsteht so kontinuierlich neue Architektur, die im Dialog mit Geschichte auch die eigene Gegenwart neu interpretiert.

Spaces in the Air

Attic conversions represent an important resource for the process of converting the city and in this context Vienna, with its substantial stock of 19th century buildings, has extensive, well-accessed reserves of space. In the constant tug-of-war between heritage authorities and plans for the sensible utilization of such spaces new architecture is constantly being created that also re-interprets its own present through a dialogue with history.

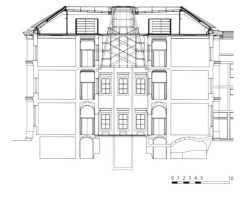

Legendäre Institution

Als das Österreichische Museum für Kunst und Industrie 1867 eine Kunstgewerbeschule gründete, befand sich das Land mitten in einem technisch-industriellen Aufholprozess, den man durch derlei fortschrittliche Institutionen stimulieren wollte. Der Kern der Kunstgewerbedebatte des 19. Jahrhunderts, nämlich die angestrebte Qualitätsverbesserung der neuen industriellen Gebrauchsgüterproduktion durch qualifizierte Formgebung, ist im weitesten Sinne immer noch Aufgabe dieser Schule. Die heutige Universität für angewandte Kunst bietet mittlerweile 1.300 Studierenden verschiedenste Studienrichtungen von Architektur über Bildende Kunst bis zur Pädagogik. Der dauernde Expansionsprozess dieser traditionsreichen Institution, an der einst Größen wie Josef Hoffmann, Oskar Kokoschka, Heinrich Tessenow, Josef Frank und Hans Hollein lehrten (heute findet sich hier das Star-Trio Wolf Prix, Zaha Hadid und Greg Lynn), stand einer ebenso zähen bürokratischen Behinderung durch die staatliche Verwaltung gegenüber. Heinrich von Ferstels erster Schulbauentwurf wurde kurz vor der Ausführung 1877 radikal zurechtgestutzt, Josef Hoffmanns Erweiterungspläne der Zeit um 1900 ignoriert, ein rückseitiger Zubau zum alten

Legendary Institution

When the Austrian Museum for Art and Industry set up a school of applied arts in 1867 the country was striving to catch up with other nations, both technically and industrially, and it was hoped that progressive institutions of this kind would advance this process. The core of the applied art debate in the 19th century, i.e. the aim of improving the quality of new, industrially made everyday goods by means of qualified form-giving remains, in the broadest sense, the aim of the school. The present-day University of Applied Arts offers 1,300 students various courses ranging from architecture to fine art to pedagogics. The continuous expansion of this venerable institution, where major figures such as Josef Hoffmann, Oskar Kokoschka, Heinrich Tessenow, Josef Frank and Hans Hollein taught (and where today the star trio Wolf Prix, Zaha Hadid and Greg Lynn teach), has always encountered bureaucratic obstacles placed in its way by the sluggish imperial administration. Heinrich von Ferstel's first design for the school was radically reduced in size shortly before start of construction in 1877, Josef Hoffmann's expansion plans for the period around 1900 were ignored, a new building at the back of the old building on the Ringstrasse was erected only in the 1960s and was, in any case, far too small. Since that date the recent attic conversion of the Ferstel wing is the first construction project worth mentioning that gives the university (which for decades has had to rent additional accommodation for its numerous branches in nearby areas of the city) tangible additional space, although it still does not represent the definitive solution to the perennial shortage of space.

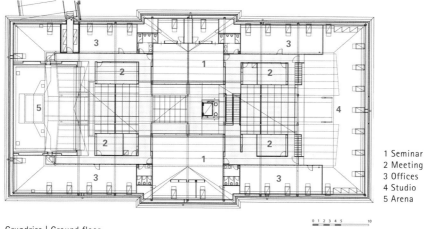

1 Seminar
2 Meeting
3 Offices
4 Studio
5 Arena

Grundriss | Ground floor

0 1 2 3 4 5   10

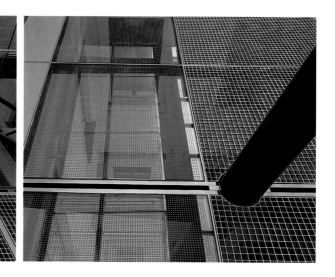

Ringstraßenhaus erst verspätet und zu gering dimensioniert in den 1960er Jahren errichtet. Der Dachausbau des Ferstel-Trakts ist seither die erste nennenswerte Baumaßnahme, die der Schule, die schon seit Jahrzehnten zahlreiche Außenstellen im näheren Stadtgebiet anmieten muss, spürbaren Raumgewinn verschafft, aber noch lange keine definitive Lösung des traditionellen Raumproblems bietet.

Klare Aussagen

Der Umbau des Ferstel-Baus beschränkte sich nicht auf den Dachausbau. Die Neuordnung beseitigte auch diverse Provisorien, die sich im Laufe von Jahrzehnten der Nutzung unter Raumnot angesammelt hatten, darunter größere Einbauten in den beiden Innenhöfen sowie die Nutzung des alten Foyers beim repräsentativen Ringstraßen-Eingang als Mensa. Dieser Eingang war in den 1960er Jahren anlässlich des ersten Zubaus in den Verbindungstrakt zwischen Ferstel- und Neubautrakt verlegt worden. Der Um- und Ausbau von Anton Falkeis ermöglicht nun durch licht- und luftdurchlässige Überdachung der alten Innenhöfe deren Integration in die Klimahülle des Hauses, wodurch sie im Erdgeschoß von allen Seiten her geöffnet und als Ausstellungsräume genutzt werden können. Vom alten Ringstraßeneingang über die offenen Innenhöfe bis zum Verbindungstrakt fließt nun eine neue, großzügige Erschließungszone, welche die Qualitäten des gründerzeitlichen Baus erst erlebbar macht.

Das neue Dachgeschoß hatte mit der Denkmalschutz-Auflage zu kämpfen, dass die äußere Erscheinung des Hauses um kein Jota verändert werden durfte. Ursprünglich sollte sogar das weniger wertvolle innere Gesperre des Dachstuhls erhalten werden, was jede sinnvolle Neunutzung ausgeschlossen hätte. In zähen Verhandlungen mit der Denkmalschutzbehörde gelang es Anton Falkeis, zumindest das freie Innenvolumen der alten Dachsilhouette als Planungsspielraum zu gewinnen. Das Tragwerk des neuen Dachs, in dem nun Büros und Seminarräume untergebracht sind, wurde als schlanke, elegante Stahlkonstruktion aus Stützenjochen im Abstand von 6,60 m mit angeschlossenen Hauptbindern und eingehängten Stahlpfetten als Tragstruktur für Glasdach und Sonnenschutz auf die alten Mauern aufgesetzt. Die Stützenjoche durchstoßen die Dachgeschoßebene und sind sichtbar in den Innenhofwänden gelagert. Tragwerksplaner Klaus Bollinger lehrt übrigens ebenso wie der Architekt selbst am Haus.

Clear Statements

The conversion of the Ferstel building is not restricted to the attic. The new layout also removed diverse provisional arrangements that had accumulated in the course of the decades under the pressure of shortage of space, including larger insertions in the two inner courtyards as well as the use of the old foyer at the imposing Ringstrasse entrance as a student canteen. In the course of the first extension in the 1960s this entrance was moved around the corner to the wing connecting the Ferstel tract with the new building. The re-planning and conversion by Anton Falkeis has integrated the old inner courtyards in the climatic shell of the building by roofing them in a way that allows the entry of light and air. In addition, the opportunity was taken to open them on all sides at ground floor level and to use them as exhibition spaces. A new, spacious circulation zone now extends from the old Ringstrasse entrance through the open courtyards to the connecting wing and allows us to experience the qualities of the 19th century building.

The new attic storey had to battle with restrictions imposed by the conservation authority with did not permit alterations that would change the exterior appearance of the building by as much as an iota. Originally, even the less important internal rafters of the roof trusses were to be preserved, which would have made any sensible new use impossible. In the course of tough negotiations with the authorities Anton Falkeis succeeded in winning at least the unobstructed volume within the existing roof silhouette as space for his design. The structure of the new roof space, in which offices and seminar rooms are located, was placed on the old walls as a slender elegant steel construction of column bents at centres of 6.60 meters with attached main beams and steel purlins to carry the glass roof and the sun screens. The column bents penetrate the attic storey to rest visibly on the internal courtyard walls. Incidentally, like the architect the structural designer, Klaus Bollinger, teaches in the University.

The outcome of this creative collaboration is a generously sized, light-flooded "centre aisle" that spans the entire length of the old building plus the inner courtyards and not only attracts new attention but, most importantly, allows more up to date ways of using the building. The offices and studio spaces are located at the sides, behind glass walls and under the slope of the roof; the seminar rooms are glass boxes

Das Ergebnis dieser kreativen Zusammenarbeit ist ein großzügig lichtdurchflutetes „Mittelschiff", das die gesamte Länge des alten Hauses samt Innenhöfen überspannt und ihm damit nicht nur neue Aufmerksamkeit, sondern vor allem zeitgemäßere Nutzungsmöglichkeiten verschafft. Büros und Studioräume sind seitlich hinter Glaswänden unter den Dachschrägen untergebracht, die Seminarräume als gläserne Boxen frei in das Mittelschiff gestellt. Eine raumbreite Holztreppe an einer Schmalseite des zentralen Freiraums dient als Sitzgelegenheit und Arena und wurde von den Studierenden auch sofort so genutzt. Die Erschließung erfolgt durch einen neuen, gläsernen Lift sowie durch zwei verglaste Treppenläufe, die sich an die Innenwand eines der Innenhöfe schmiegen und ihm so einen interessanten skulpturalen Effekt verschaffen. Viele liebevolle und aufwändige Details des Dachausbaus zeigen die gestalterische Ambition des Architekten, darunter die Beleuchtungen, die geschickt in die Teilungen von Wand- und Deckenkonstruktionen integriert und so fast unsichtbar gemacht wurden, oder auch die Materialwahl mit Glas, Stahl, Gitterrosten als Innenhofabdeckungen, durchgefärbtem Beton und Holz. So wird das konstruktive System erlebbar gemacht und eine zeitgemäßklare, angenehm sachliche Atmosphäre geschaffen.

positioned freely in the centre aisle. A wooden staircase the width of the space at one short end of the central open area is also a place to sit and this arena and was immediately taken over as such by the students. The circulation is by means a new glazed lift as well as two glazed stairs that rise along the inner wall of one of the courtyards, lending it an interesting sculptural effect. Many of the complex details of the attic conversion were worked out with a dedicated enthusiasm that demonstrates the architect's design ambitions. These include the light fittings that are so cleverly integrated in the divisions between the bays of the wall and ceiling construction that they are almost invisible, and the choice of materials – glass, steel and steel gratings that roof the inner courtyards, coloured concrete and wood. The constructional system is made clearly legible, creating a clear, pleasantly functional atmosphere that is thoroughly contemporary.

Dachgeschoß-Ausbau
Wien-Innere Stadt, Oskar Kokoschka-Platz 2

Bauherr I client **BIG Bundes Immobilien Gesellschaft**
Planung I planning **Falkeis & Falkeis-Senn Architekten**
Projektleitung I project manager **Anton Falkeis**
Mitarbeiter I assistance **Wolfgang Hirsch**
Statik I structural consultant **Bollinger + Grohmann + Schneider**
Dach/Glas I roof/glass **Fritsch Stiassny**
Stahlkonstruktion I steel structure **Urbas; SFL Metallbau; Mandl + Eckl; Binder**
Membranen I membranes **Skyspan Europe**
Brandschutztüren I fire doors **ABS + BTS**
Elektroinstallationen I electrical services **Grissenberger**
Heizung/Lüftung/Klima I heating/ventilation/air conditioning **Caliqua**
Lichtausstattung I lighting fittings **SITECO**
Böden I flooring **Mörtinger**
Möbel I furnishings **Donner**
Aufzug I elevator **DIMA; Haushahn**

Nutzfläche I floor area	1.800 m²
Wettbewerb I competition	1999
Baubeginn I start of construction	2002
Fertigstellung I completion	2004

RATAPLAN

Kulturzentrum Arena Wien
Arena Culture Centre, Vienna

Photos Peter Bittermann, Markus Tomaselli
Text Robert Temel

Das Erbe der Besetzer

Das Architekturatelier RATAPLAN arbeitet seit 1995 am schrittweisen Umbau des seit der Besetzung in den 1970er Jahren legendären Wiener Kulturzentrums „Arena" in Erdberg, im November 2004 wurde die zweite Etappe fertig gestellt. Weitere Etappen für die Adaption einer kleinen Halle, für Seminar- und Verwaltungsräume sind in naher Zukunft geplant, aber noch nicht finanziert.

Squatters' Heritage

The architecture studio RATAPLAN has been working since 1995 on the phased conversion of the "Arena", the legendary culture centre in Vienna since the sit-in in the 1970s. The second phase was completed in November 2004. Further stages, including the adaptation of a small hall and seminar and administration spaces, are planned for the near future but financing has not yet been secured.

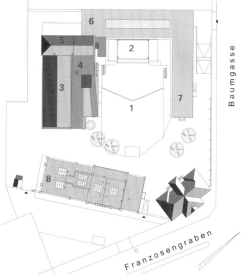

1 Open Air Gelände | Open air site
2 Open Air Bühne | Open air stage
3 Große Halle | Big hall
4 Große Halle Zubau | Big hall addition
5 Graues Haus | Grey house
6 Durchfahrtshalle | Access hall
7 Ostflügel | East wing
8 Kleine Halle | Small hall

Das Erbe der Arenauten

Im legendären heißen Sommer 1976 sollte der Auslandsschlachthof St. Marx (70.000 m² groß) das letzte Mal für die Veranstaltungsreihe „Arena" der Festwochen genützt und dann abgerissen werden – die „Arenauten", mehrere Künstlergruppen und ihr Publikum, versuchten, das mit einer Besetzung zu verhindern. Die Besetzer hielten den Sommer über stand, dann wurde geräumt und abgerissen, doch bot die Stadt Wien als Alternative den nahe gelegenen Inlandsschlachthof, der nur etwa 7.600 m² groß ist. Mehr oder weniger besetzungsartig begann dort 1977 ein Kulturbetrieb, der unter dem Druck einer „neuen" Jugendbewegung ab 1980 seine Legalisierung erreichte. Seit nahezu 30 Jahren läuft also der Betrieb in den teils schon damals in schlechtem Zustand befindlichen Gebäuden. Adaptierungen wurden immer nur per Selbstbau vorgenommen – allerdings macht genau dieser leicht verkommene Zustand auch einen wesentlichen Reiz der Arena aus. Beim aktuellen Umbau, finanziert von der Stadt Wien, musste darauf Rücksicht genommen werden, dass die Arenabesucher das Areal am liebsten unverändert hätten. Eine Architektur mit perfekten Details und glatten Oberflächen würden sie niemals akzeptieren – dementsprechend ist es Teil des architektonischen Konzeptes von RATAPLAN, das Gebäude in einem „halbfertigen" Zustand zu übergeben, sodass der Endausbau wieder in Eigenregie erfolgen kann.

The Inheritance of the „Arenauten"

In the legendary hot summer of 1976 the St Marx export abattoir measuring 70,000 square metres in area was to be used for a final time for the "Arena" events that formed of the Wiener Festwochen (Vienna summer festival) and then demolished. The "Arenauten", several artists' groups and their public attempted to prevent this by occupying the building. The squatters kept up their resistance over the summer but they were finally cleared out and the demolition work started. But the Vienna municipal authorities offered them the nearby domestic abattoir which was only around 7,600 square metres in area. Cultural activities started there in 1977, more of less in the form of a squat, which under the pressure of a "new" youth movement achieved legal status from 1980 onwards. So for almost 30 years these cultural facilities have been operating in buildings, which even back then were in poor condition. The people who ran the facilities regularly carried out provisional adaptations themselves – but in fact a slightly down-at-heel quality has always formed part of the attraction of the Arena. The current conversion financed by the Vienna municipal authorities had to take into account that most visitors to the Arena don't want anything changed: they would never accept an architecture with perfect details and smooth surfaces and consequently part of the architectural concept of RATAPLAN is to hand over the building in a "semi-complete" condition, so that final works can be carried out by the Arena people themselves.

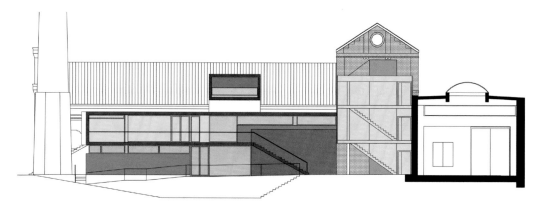

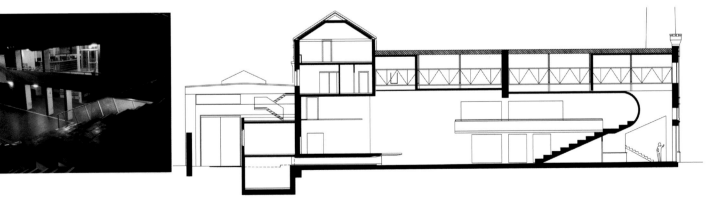

1 Foyer
2 Garderobe | Wardrobe
3 Zuschauerraum | Spectators' hall
4 Bühne | Stage
5 Zuschauerraum | Spectators' hall

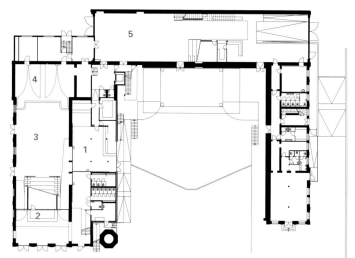

Erdgeschoß | ground floor

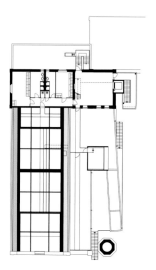

2. Obergeschoß | 2nd floor

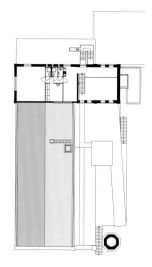

3. Obergeschoß | 3rd floor

Subkultur und Denkmalschutz

Nachdem in den 1990er Jahren die Maßnahmen vor allem in Verbesserungen für die Sicherheit und den Schallschutz bestanden hatten, etwa einer Absenkung des Open-Air-Geländes und Lärmschutzmauern, sollten nun, im zweiten Bauabschnitt, die Betriebsbedingungen für die Konzerthalle verbessert werden. Früher befanden sich Halleneingang, Bühne und Bühnenzugang an derselben Stelle, was den Betrieb massiv erschwerte. Die Verkehrswege mussten also entflochten werden. RATAPLAN schlugen vor, eine neue Bühne ans andere Ende der historischen Halle zu bauen, die dort problemlos mit dem nötigen technischen und organisatorischen Hinterland ausgestattet werden konnte, während der Eingang am alten Ort bleiben sollte und nun durch ein großes Foyer unter der neuen, geschwungenen Tribüne hindurch in die Halle läuft – die Kapazität der Konzerthalle konnte so auf 900 Personen verdoppelt werden. Der Umbau bei vollem Betrieb war nur möglich, weil eine bisher als Ruine leer stehende Halle für den zwischenzeitlichen Konzertbetrieb adaptiert worden war, allerdings so, dass Sattelschlepper durch diese „Durchfahrtshalle" hinter die neue Hauptbühne gelangen können. An Stelle eines ebenfalls ruinösen Traktes ergänzten RATAPLAN die neue Haupthalle durch einen Baukörper mit Foyers, Bars und Beisl, einer Terrasse, die zur Open-Air-Bühne orientiert ist, sowie einem neuen Kinovorführraum. Die bestehenden Bauten von 1908/09, teils denkmalgeschützt, sind durchwegs in sichtbarem Klinker ausgeführt, dem entsprechend sollten die neuen Bauteile einerseits ebenfalls ihre Materialität zeigen und sich andererseits deutlich vom Bestand abheben – so wurden Oberflächen aus Sichtbeton, Stahl und Glas verwendet, nur in den Hallen selbst musste jede Materialästhetik einem schwarzen Anstrich weichen.

Subculture and the Protection of Listed Buildings

In the 1990s the measures consisted primarily of improving the safety and the noise protection for example by lowering the open-air site and erecting noise barriers, in the second phase the aim was to improve the facilities for running the concert hall. Previously the entrance to the hall, the stage and approach to the stage were all at the same position, which made holding concerts very difficult. It was necessary to disentangle the various circulation routes. RATAPLAN proposed building a new stage at the far end of the historic hall which could be simply provided with the necessary technical and organisational facilities, while the entrance remained at its old position and now extends into the hall through a large foyer under a new curved spectator stand – these moves doubled the capacity of the hall to 900 persons. It was possible to carry out the building works while still holding concerts because a building that had been an empty ruin was adapted as a provisional concert hall in such a way that articulated trucks could drive through this „access hall" behind the new main stage. In place of another, equally desolate wing RATAPLAN extended the new main hall with an element containing foyers, bars and restaurant, a terrace oriented towards the open-air stage, as well as a new cinema projection room. The existing buildings from 1908/09, some of which are under a preservation order are all made of exposed brickwork, accordingly the new building elements also display their materials while still clearly distinguish themselves from the existing fabric – the surfaces are exposed concrete, steel and glass, but inside the halls themselves aesthetic notions about materials were subjected to a coat of black paint!

Arena Wien
Wien-St. Marx, Baumgasse 80

Bauherr | client **MA 34, Bau- & Gebäudemanagement**
Planung | planning **RATAPLAN**
Mitarbeiter | assistance **Otto Arnold, Waltraud Hoheneder, Benjamin Lehner, Julian Kerschbaumer, Martha Wolzt, Katharina Müller**
Statik | structural consultant **Dipl. Ing. Ewald Pachler**
Terrassenplatten | terrace slabs **Ebenseer Betonwerke GmbH**
Glaser | glazier **Fritsch Stiassny Glastechnik GmbH**
Stahltüren | steel doors **Tortec Brandschutztor GmbH**
Elektroinstallationen | electrical services **Licht Loidl GmbH**
Sanitäre Installationen | plumbing **Instabloc**
Heizung/Lüftung/Klima | heating/ventilation/air conditioning **Stampfl & Co GmbH**
Aufzug | elevators **KONE AG; Weigl Aufzüge GmbH & Co KG**
Bühnentechnik | stage technique **Franz Tüchler GmbH**

Grundstücksfläche | site area	7.600 m²
Nutzfläche/Open Airgelände | open air area	ca. 1.400 m²
Nutzfläche/Große Halle | floor area/grand hall	1.430 m²
Bebaute Fläche/Große Halle | built-up area/grand hall	947 m²
Umbauter Raum/Große Halle | cubage/grand hall	8.345 m³
Nutzfläche/Durchfahrtshalle | floor area/transit hall	505 m²
Bebaute Fläche/Durchfahrtshalle | built-up area/transit hall	562 m²
Umbauter Raum/Durchfahrtshalle | cubage/transit hall	4.345 m³
Planungsbeginn | start of planning	11/1994
Baubeginn | start of construction	8/1997
Fertigstellung | completion	11/2004
Baukosten | building costs	3,5 Mio EUR

EOOS

A1 Lounge/Flagship Store, Wien | Vienna

Photos Hans Georg Esch, Paul Prader
Text Elke Krasny

Science Fiction-Poesie

Warenpräsentation und Einkaufs-Räume haben in
den letzten Jahren vehement an gestalterischer Dimension gewonnen. Selten jedoch wurde die Inter-
pretation einer eigentlich virtuellen Verkaufssituati-
on, wie die eines Telefonie-Anbieters, A1 Mobilkom
Austria, so intelligent und im Wesen des Produkts
agierend interpretiert wie von der in Wien arbeiten-
den, international auf Flagship Stores spezialisierten
Designergruppe EOOS.

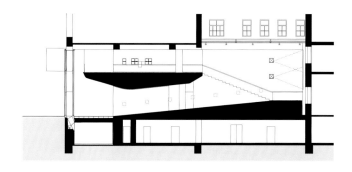

The Poetry of Science Fiction

In recent years the presentation of goods and sales spaces has dramatically acquired quality design
dimensions. It is, however, rare that a virtual sales situation (in this case for the telephone provider,
A1 Mobilkom Austria) is so intelligently interpreted, with such a true understanding of the nature of
the product, as is shown here by the Vienna-based designer group EOOS — specialists in the design
of international flagship stores.

Eine poetische Analyse stand am Anfang, Science Fiction-Filme lieferten das symbolische Bild. So technoid das hier gebotene Produkt und die Gestaltung sind, so wenig spürbar wird die Technik, deren reibungsloses Funktionieren gut verborgen im Hintergrund bleibt. Alle Details tragen die Handschrift von EOOS, alle Ausstattungselemente bis zur Türklinke.

Die Hauptfassade zur Mariahilferstraße, in der Verlängerung sieht man den Flakturm im Esterhazypark, wird einmal stündlich in anders farbigen Nebel gehüllt, die dazugehörige Maschine auf einer Effektmesse in Dubai entdeckt. Die nuancenreichen Lichtlösungen wurden in einem Entwicklungsprozess mit Zumtobel Staff realisiert. Wie überhaupt eine Fülle von Wissen aus unterschiedlichen Sparten in der Gesamterscheinung steckt. Das Personal ist von Schella Kann eingekleidet, die Sounds stammen von Virgil Widrich. Unter einem silbernen Blechfügel geht man die Zukunftsrampe hinauf, an deren Ende beim überdachten Lichthof eine interaktive Installation des Ars Electronica Center über digitale Sensoren die Besucherbewegungen abnimmt. Diese werden als abstrakte, ästhetische Muster projiziert. Mini-Holodecks in Form von kleinen, von der Wand abstehenden Boxen entlang der Rampe liefern über handgeschliffene, polierte Hohlspiegel Hologramme zukünftiger Produkte. Im Obergeschoß finden sich die schwarz-weiße Lounge sowie ein durch eine Schiebewand abtrennbarer Konferenzraum. Größte Herausforderung waren die Verkaufstische, denen man im Foyer erstmals begegnet und die im Untergeschoß die Hauptakteure sind. Die Ungegenständlichkeit dessen, was man hier kauft, Zugang zu einem Telefonnetz, Klingeltöne, Serviceleistungen, inkarniert sich in einem kleinen kristallinen Körper: dem „gläsernen" Handy. Mit diesem in der Hand dockt man sich an die Laptops der Verkaufstische an, ausgestattet mit echten Handys, speichert die Daten seiner Wahl, und trägt sie zur Kasse. Ein Technologiemuseum sollte diese prototypische Shopvision nicht werden, aber technische Museen könnten sich vom intelligenten Medieneinsatz einiges abschauen.

The start was a poetic analysis; science fiction films provided the symbolic image. Although the product offered and the designs are highly technical in nature, the technology is barely perceptible; it functions without a hitch, concealed in the background. All the details and all the fittings down to the door handles carry the stamp of EOOS.

The main façade is onto Mariahilfer Strasse, a busy shopping street (a WW II anti-aircraft defence tower in the Esterhazy Park lies on the axis of the shop). It is shrouded in a differently coloured mist at hourly intervals. The machinery responsible was discovered at a special effects trade fair in Dubai. The subtle lighting solutions were developed in conjunction with Zumtobel Staff. Indeed a wealth of knowledge from various branches is contained in the overall appearance of the premises. The staff is dressed by Schella Kann, the sounds are from Virgil Widrich. Under a silvery metal wing you ascend the future ramp that ends at a roofed light well where an interactive installation from the Ars Electronica reacts by means of digital sensors to the movements of the visitors, projecting them as abstract, aesthetic patterns. Mini holodecks in the form of small boxes projecting from the wall beside the ramp present holograms of future projects on hand-polished hollow mirrors. On the upper floor is a black and white lounge as well as a conference room that can be closed off by a sliding wall. The sales counters, which you first encounter in the foyer and which are the main protagonists on the lower ground floor level, presented a major challenge. The abstract quality of what is sold here – access to a telephone network, ring tones for mobile phones and various services – is embodied in a small crystalline element: the transparent mobile phone. With this in your hand you can connect with laptops on the sales counters that are equipped with real mobile phones, you save the data of your choice and bring them to the cash desk. It is not intended that this vision of a prototype shop should become a technology museum but it is true that technical museums could learn a great deal from the intelligent use that this project makes of media.

a1 lounge
Wien-Neubau, Mariahilferstraße 60

Bauherr I client **mobilkom austria**
Generalunternehmer I building contractor **Construction Support BaugmbH**
Planung I planning **EOOS**
Projektleitung I project manager **mobilkom austria; Project**
Statik I structural consultant **Dipl. Ing. Pfeil**
Fassaden I facade **Construction Support BaugmbH**
Dach/Stahlkonstruktion I roof/steel structure **WiBA; F. X. Jäger**
Böden I flooring **Rhode; Goldbach**
Fenster/glasfassade I windows/glass facade **Pilkington; Hanausek**
Schiebetüren I sliding doors **GEZE GmbH**
Elektroinstallationen I electrical services **Rugovaj OEG; Doskoczil + Meissl OEG**
Heizung/Lüftung/Klima/Sanitäre Installationen I
    heating/ventilation/air conditioning/plumbing **Ing. Haas GmbH**
Lichtplanung/-ausstattung I lighting concept/fittings **Zumtobel Staff; Luxmate**
Möbel I furnishings **Walter Knoll**
Sonnenschutz I sun protection **Silent Gliss**
Sound **Ceckpoint Media**
Security **PKE Electronics AG**
Nebelmaschine I fog machine **MT-Electronics**
Multimedia **3C Creative Compoting Concepts; Compitence IT Solution**

Nutzfläche I floor area	ca. 700 m²
Planungsbeginn I start of planning	11/2003
Baubeginn I start of construction	2/2004
Fertigstellung I completion	7/2004

Stadtgestalt und Stadtentwicklung Wien 2005
The Shape of the City and Urban Development 2005

Robert Temel

Stadtentwicklung – Stadtgestalt

Stadtentwicklung ist ein Handlungsfeld, das sich nicht nur, aber auch mit der Stadtgestalt befasst. Der Grundgedanke der Gestalttheorie wurde von ihrem Begründer Max Wertheimer in den 1920er Jahren etwa so formuliert: Es bestehen Zusammenhänge, bei denen sich das Ganze nicht nur aus der Art und der Zusammensetzung der Einzelteile ergibt, sondern wo umgekehrt alle Teile von Strukturgesetzen des Ganzen bestimmt sind – das bedeutet, die Eigenschaften des Ganzen können nicht einfach aus denen der Teile erschlossen werden. Von diesem psychologisch-philosophischem Zugang in die urbane Praxis gehend, kann man auch die Stadtgestalt so bestimmt sehen. Sie setzt sich zusammen aus einem breiten Spektrum verschiedenster Elemente, vom kleinsten der Stadtmöblierung bis zum größten des Stadtpanoramas. Und doch ist das Ergebnis, die Gestalt der Stadt, die ihre Bewohner und Benützer in ihrer Vorstellung im ständigen Austausch mit den Phänomenen der Realität erzeugen, mehr als nur die Summe dieser Elemente. Kleine Änderungen an Details können gravierende Auswirkungen haben, während andere Elemente so robust sind, dass auch ihre völlige Veränderung sich im Ganzen kaum bemerkbar macht. Und umgekehrt gibt es Teile der Stadtgestalt, die von fast allen Stadtbenützern ziemlich gleich wahrgenommen werden, während andere Teile jeder anders sieht. Die Stadtgestalt besitzt jedenfalls nicht rein visuellen Charakter, sondern eine Fülle sinnlicher und atmosphärischer, funktionaler und sozialer Eigenschaften trägt mit zum Ganzen bei.

Der Wiener Stadtentwicklungsplan

Bereits seit den 1980er Jahren wird alle zehn Jahre ein neuer Stadtentwicklungsplan für Wien erstellt, der aktuelle STEP 05 wurde im Mai 2005 vom Gemeinderat beschlossen (siehe S. 32). Erstmals endet sein Betrachtungsbereich nicht an den Stadtgrenzen, sondern bezieht das Umland und die Nachbarstadt Bratislava mit ein. Der Stadtentwicklungsplan nennt insgesamt 13 Zielgebiete, in denen in den kommenden Jahren „eine hohe Aufmerksamkeit der Stadt erforderlich sein wird" – die Auswahl reicht von innerstädtischen, gründerzeitlich bestimmten Bereichen bis zur viel zitierten „grünen Wiese", für die eine baldige Entwicklung erwartet wird. Dabei sind sehr

Urban Development – Shaping the City

Urban development is an area of activity that deals with the form, shape or appearance (in German "Gestalt") of the city but also with far more than this. The basic concept of Gestalt theory as formulated by its founder Max Wertheimer in the 1920s is more or less as follows: there are relationships and contexts in which the whole is not only the product of the parts and the way they are put together but where, conversely, all the parts are determined by the structural laws governing the whole – this means that the qualities of the whole cannot simply be grasped from those of the parts. Taking this psychological and philosophical approach to urban practice as a starting point one can view the form or shape of the city in much the same way. It is composed of a wide range of very disparate elements, from the smallest pieces of street furniture to the large elements of the urban panorama. And yet the result, the appearance of the city that its residents and users produce in their imagination through a constant process of exchange with the phenomena of reality, is more than merely the sum of these elements. Small alterations to details can have serious effects, whereas other elements are so robust that even changing them completely has little overall effect. And, in contrast, there are parts of the urban form that almost all users of the city register in much the same way, whereas other parts are seen differently by each individual. The form of the city certainly does not have a purely visual character, a wealth of sensual and atmospheric, functional and social qualities combine to form the whole.

The Vienna Urban Development Plan

Starting back in the 1980s, a new urban development plan for Vienna has been prepared every ten years, the current such plan, STEP 05, was passed by the municipal council in May 2005 (see p. 32). For the first time the area dealt with in the plan does not end at the city boundaries but includes the surrounding areas and the neighbouring city of Bratislava. The urban development plan lists a total of 13 target areas to which, in the coming years, "concentrated attention will have to be paid by the city". The areas selected range from inner city, predominantly 19th century areas to the often-mentioned

Zaha Hadid
Apartments Spittelauer Lände
PHOTOS BRUNO KLOMFAR

131

viele Variablen zu berücksichtigen, sodass sich im Laufe der etwa zehn Jahre zwischen zwei Plänen vieles ändern kann. Beispielsweise ist bis heute unklar, ob in Rothneusiedl an der Wiener Südgrenze eine massivere Entwicklung zu erwarten ist – aber das Areal ist schon mal zu einem Zielgebiet erklärt, und die nächste Ausbaustufe der U-Bahn sieht eine Verlängerung dorthin vor. Neu am STEP 05 ist auch, dass erstmals ein dezidiertes Instrumentarium für eine Evaluation der Steuerungseffekte vorgesehen ist, die sich vor allem auch auf die Pläne für die Zielgebiete bezieht.

Parallel zu den Zielgebieten werden im STEP 05 so genannte „Potenzialflächen für größere Stadtentwicklungsprojekte" ausgewiesen, die anhand einer stadträumlichen Typologie geordnet sind. Es handelt sich dabei um innerstädtische Flächen, Areale für innere Stadterweiterung, Bürokonzentrationen außerhalb des Zentrums sowie Siedlungsachsen als Felder der „äußeren" Stadterweiterung und, diesen angelagert, außerhalb liegende Regionalzentren. Schließlich, separiert von den Linien einer verdichtenden Entwicklung, folgen noch grüne Wohngebiete, Gewerbeparks und umzunutzende ehemalige Gewerbeflächen. Diese Typologisierung zusammen mit den Zielgebieten bietet das ganze Spektrum der Möglichkeiten der Stadtentwicklung, von Stadterneuerung über innere bis zur „äußeren" Stadterweiterung. Es zeigt sich dabei aber auch, dass es nicht mehr möglich ist, eine dieser Strategien zulasten anderer in den Vordergrund zu stellen. Die Rahmenbedingungen heutiger Stadtentwicklungsplanung, die den Spielraum für Politik und Verwaltung zunehmend reduzieren, etablieren andere Entscheidungsgrundlagen als derartig strategische. So kommt es, dass riesige innerstädtische Flächen wie der Nordbahnhof sich mit unglaublicher Langsamkeit weiterentwickeln, während gleichzeitig weit draußen, wo keine vergleichbare Erschließung besteht, neue Stadtteile entstehen.

Als dritte Perspektive der Betrachtung neben Zielgebieten und Flächentypologie führt der STEP 05 schließlich noch eine Zusammenschau des räumlichen Leitbildes ein, in der die wichtigsten Entwicklungsgebiete der Zeit bis 2010 und danach genannt werden. Dabei handelt es sich kurzfristig um Erdberger Mais/Simmering, also das Gasometer-Umfeld, um die Linie Donaukanal-Praterstern-Messegelände und Stadlau-Aspern entlang der verlängerten U2, und um die Linie Kagran-Großfeldsiedlung entlang der verlängerten U1. Nach 2010 stehen das Gebiet des Flugfelds Aspern und das Areal um den geplanten Bahnhof Wien – Europa Mitte im Zentrum – zumindest war das noch Stand der Dinge im Mai 2005.

Investorenstädtebau

Aktuell in Diskussion sind allerdings andere Gebiete, deren Nutzung schon weiter fortgeschritten ist und deren Standortwahl in keiner Weise einem Stadtentwicklungsplan oder ähnlichen Instrumenten des öffentlichen Interesses entstammt, sondern vorrangig dem Vorteil des Grundeigentümers verpflichtet ist. Deshalb wurde für derartige Projekte der Begriff Investorenstädtebau geprägt, der sich nicht nur darauf bezieht, dass das jeweilige Projekt von privaten Investoren realisiert wird, sondern dass die Standortwahl nicht Anforderungen der Allgemeinheit genügt. Dabei handelt es sich um die neuen Stadtteile am Wienerberg, wo die Entwicklung praktisch abgeschlossen ist, und am Laaer Berg, bekannt unter dem Namen Monte Laa. Im STEP 05 ist deutlich sichtbar, auf welche Weise sich diese Projekte von allen anderen in Wien unterscheiden: Beim Thema Bürostandorte außerhalb des Zentrums sind insgesamt zehn derartige Entwicklungen angeführt, von denen alle bis auf diese beiden eine hochrangige, das heißt mittels U-Bahn realisierte Anbindung an den öffentlichen Verkehr und ebenso an den Individualverkehr besitzen. Der STEP 05 schlägt des-

greenfield areas, where development is expected to take place shortly. Hereby a great number of variables must be taken into account, which means that a great deal can change in the course of the ten-year period that elapses between two plans. For example, it is still unclear whether massive development is to be expected in Rothneusiedl on Vienna's southern boundary – but the area has already been declared a target zone and there are plans to extend the Underground railway there in the transport authority's next development phase. Another new feature of STEP 05 is that, for the first time ever, a definite set of instruments is proposed that will help evaluate its influences and effects, this evaluation will focus above all on the plans for the target areas.

Parallel to the target areas in STEP 05 so-called "potential areas for larger urban development, projects" are designated and listed according to a typology of urban areas. This list includes inner city areas, areas for inner urban expansion, concentrations of office space outside the centre, as well as settlement axes as fields for "outer" urban expansion and, attached to the latter, outer regional centres. Finally, separated from the lines of compressed development, are the green residential areas, commercial parks and those former industrial areas awaiting conversion. Together with the target areas this typological classification offers an entire spectrum of possibilities in the field of urban development, from urban renewal to inner and "outer" urban expansion. In the process it is also revealed that it is no longer possible to give one of these possibilities priority over the others in a strategic way. The outline conditions of present day urban development, which are increasingly reducing the leeway available to politics and the urban administration, are establishing bases for decision-making very different to these strategic concepts. Thus enormous inner city areas, such as the Nordbahnhof (North Railway Station), are developing at a snail-like pace, while at the same time, far outside the city at locations with comparatively poor access, new urban districts are rapidly being created.

As a third possible perspective in addition to the target zones and typological classification of areas mentioned above, STEP 05 presents a summary of the overall spatial concept in which the most important development areas of the period up to 2010 and after are named. These are, in the immediate term Erdberger Mais/Simmering, i.e. the area around the gasometers, the line Donaukanal-Praterstern-Messegelände, Stadlau-Aspern along the extended U2, and the line Kagran-Großfeldsiedlung along the extended U1. After 2010 the area around Aspern airfield and the area around the planned new central railway station Wien – Europa Mitte (Vienna - Europe Central) will form the focus – at least that was the plan in May 2005.

Urban Planning by Investors

But in the current discussion there are other, more topical areas where utilization has advanced further and where the choice of location is in no way based on an urban development plan or similar instruments of public policy but primarily serves the interests of the particular real estate owner. The term investors urban planning has been coined to describe such projects. This term refers not only to the fact that the respective projects are carried out by private investors but also to the fact that the choice of location was not dictated by the requirements of the general public. Such areas include the new urban districts at Wienerberg, where the development is practically complete, and at Laaer Berg, known as Monte Laa. STEP 05 reveals clearly how these projects differ from all others in Vienna: in the theme of office space location outside the central area a total of ten such developments are

Coop Himmelb(l)au
Apartments Schlachthausgasse
PHOTOS ANNA BLAU

halb vor, die beiden Areale mit Straßenbahnen zu erschließen, die langfristige U-Bahnplanung sieht sogar die Verlängerung der U2 bis zum Wienerberg und der U1 in die Nähe von Monte Laa vor.

Doch damit enden nicht die Probleme derartiger Projekte. Am Wienerberg ist zwar eine Reihe durchaus anspruchsvoller architektonischer Beiträge versammelt, ob nun Massimiliano Fuksas' Twin Towers, Delugan-Meissls City Lofts oder Günter Lautners Hängende Gärten, doch scheint deren Realisierung durch keinerlei städtebaulichen Rahmen geordnet zu sein. Dies führt dazu, dass erstens die Außenräume zu Abstandsflächen degeneriert sind und dass zweitens die Wohnbauten viel zu dicht aneinander stehen, um den Wohnungen noch ausreichend Licht und Sicht bieten zu können - was natürlich die Bewohner der an der Spitze der Hochhäuser liegenden, privat finanzierten Eigentumswohnungen nicht weiter stört. Das Projekt Monte Laa lässt jedenfalls in dieser Hinsicht Besseres erwarten: Die Gesamtanlage gliedert sich in einen südlichen Büroteil, in dem bisher nur zwei Projekte realisiert wurden, während der Rest inklusive der spektakulären Hochhäuser von Hans Hollein auf eine Besserung des Marktes wartet, und in einen nördlichen Wohnteil. Die Wohnbauten sind teils bereits bezogen und werden mit Ende 2006 vollständig fertig gestellt sein. Die beiden Zonen sind durch einen schmalen, lang gezogenen Parkstreifen getrennt, der auf ein Bewusstsein für die Notwendigkeit der Gestaltung auch der Räume zwischen den Investitionsobjekten schließen lässt. Mit dem Entwurf dieses Außenraums wurde die amerikanische Landschaftsplanerin Martha Schwartz beauftragt, die Detailplanung stammt von 3:0 Landschaftsarchitekten. Allerdings muss dieser gestaltete Außenraum einiges an Kompensation dafür leisten, dass die gesamte Anlage direkt an einer der meistbefahrenen Autobahnabschnitte Österreichs liegt. Fragen des hochwertigen Wohnbaus, der Bau- und Siedlungstypen für das Wohnen in der oder am Rande der Stadt oder der wohnungsbezogenen Freiräume stehen bei derartigen Projekten naturgemäß nicht im Mittelpunkt.

Hoch und niedrig

Die beiden beschriebenen Projekte, Wienerberg und Monte Laa, beziehen ihr Bild als Stadtteile der Zukunft vor allem auch daraus, dass Hochhäuser wesentliche Teile des Ensembles sind. Bei Fuksas' bis zu 140 Meter hohen Twin Towers liegt die architektonische Qualität jedenfalls höher als beim durchschnittlichen Wiener Hochhausbau, bei Holleins Porr-Türmen von 110 Meter Höhe bleibt das noch abzuwarten. Hochhaus-Cluster wie die Donau-City mitsamt der Zone entlang der Wagramer Straße oder die Wienerberg-City sind jedenfalls ein wichtiger Typus des zeitgenössischen Hochhausbaus, dessen erstes Ergebnis Wilhelm Holzbauers Andromeda-Tower von 1997 mit 100 Metern war - dazu könnte man auch die Hochhausreihe entlang des Donaukanals in der Leopoldstadt zählen. Dem entgegen steht der Typus des Einzelturmes: Wie die Praxis zeigt, kann auch ein einzelnes Hochhaus besser (Millennium Tower) und schlechter (Florido Tower) platziert sein. Neue Einzelturmprojekte gibt es beispielsweise für die Kometgründe in Meidling und die Krieau. Wiener Cluster-Hochhausplanungen stehen in der Donau-City, in TownTown in Erdberg, am Anfang der Taborstraße (Uniqa) und am Südbahnhofareal an. Nicht zu vergessen das neue Projekt von Henke-Schreieck für Wien Mitte, das niedriger als das alte ist und mit einem einzigen Hochhaus auskommt. Mit dem bereits realisierten City Tower wird so die Reihe vom Donaukanal kommend entlang der Wien fortgesetzt, was jedenfalls für den Standort Wien Mitte, einen wichtigen Verkehrsknotenpunkt der Stadt, sicherlich sinnvoll ist.

listed, all of which – except for these two – have a highly efficient connection to the public transport system (i.e. a connection by Underground), as well as to the private transport network. STEP 05 therefore proposes accessing both these sites with a tram line and the long-term plan for the Underground even envisages extending the U2 line to Wienerberg and the U1 to near Monte Laa.

But this is not an end to the problems of such projects. Although at Wienerberg a series of ambitious architectural projects has been created, including the Twin Towers by Massimiliano Fuksas, Delugan Meissl's City Lofts and Günter Lautners Hanging Gardens, these projects do not seem to be organised within any urban planning framework. This deficit leads to the outdoor spaces degenerating to spaces in-between and also means that the residential buildings are far too close to each other to offer all dwellings sufficient light and views – which does not greatly worry those living at the top of the blocks in the privately financed and owned apartments. In this respect the Monte Laa project at least offers more reason for hope. The entire complex is articulated into a southern office area (where to date only two projects have been completed, while the rest of the designs, including a spectacular high-rise building by Hans Hollein, await an improvement in the property market), and a northern residential area. Some of the residential blocks are already occupied and this area will be completed by the end of 2006. The two zones are separated by a narrow, elongated strip of parkland that suggests an awareness of the necessity to apply design to the spaces between buildings also. American landscape planner Martha Schwartz was commissioned as designer of this outdoor space, the detail planning is by 3:0 landscape architects. However, this outdoor space must attempt to offer compensation for the fact that the entire complex stands on one the busiest sections of motorway in Austria. In this kind of project questions about high-quality housing design, the types of buildings and housing estates suitable for living in the city or on its perimeter, or the issue of outdoor space in relation to housing are, naturally, not a central issue.

Hi-rise and low

The two projects described above, Wienerberg and Monte Laa, derive their image as urban districts of the future primarily from the fact that in both cases high-rise blocks form a prominent feature of the ensemble. In the case of Fuksas' Twin Towers, which reach a height of 140 metres, the architectural quality is considerably higher than that of the average Viennese high-rise block, with Hollein's planned Porr Towers (height 110 metres) the outcome must still be awaited. Clusters of high-rise buildings such as the Donau City with the zone along Wagramer Straße, or the Wienerberg City are an important type of contemporary high-rise development. The first building in such a cluster was Wilhelm Holzbauer's 100-metre-high Andromeda Tower (1997). The row of high-rise buildings along the Danube Canal in the Leopoldstadt district of Vienna could be included in this series. The individual freestanding tower provides a contrasting example: practice has shown that a single high-rise can be positioned well (Millenium Tower) or badly (Florido Tower). New solitary tower projects are planned for the Komet Grounds in Meidling and for Krieau. High-rise clusters are proposed for the Donau City, in TownTown in Erdberg, at the beginning of Taborstraße (Uniqa insurance company) and around the Südbahnhof railway station. In this context the new project by architects Henke-Schreieck for Wien Mitte should not be forgotten, it is lower than the original project and has only a single high-rise element. Together with the already completed City Tower the Wien Mitte project will continue a series that starts at the Danube Canal along the River Wien, which certainly makes

Carl Pruscha
MQ West office building
PHOTOS ANNA BLAU

Gustav Peichl & Partner
Toscanahof apartments, Argentinierstraße

ARTEC
Wohnhaus | Housing development Alxingergasse

Geiswinkler-Geiswinkler Architekten
Wohnhaus | Housing development Alxingergasse/Hardtmuthgasse
PHOTOS MANFRED SEIDEL

Wien ist im europäischen Kontext eine erstaunlich aktive Hochhausstadt. Andere bedeutende Städte in Europa, die auf Hochhäuser setzen, sind Warschau und Moskau, wo in jüngster Zeit sehr viele Hochhäuser gebaut werden, Paris, wo sich die Wolkenkratzer heute auf La Défense außerhalb der Stadt beschränken, Frankfurt mit dem innerstädtischen Bankencluster sowie London – während in London lange Zeit Hochhäuser hauptsächlich fern der City in Canary Wharf entstanden, scheint sich nun, spätestens seit Norman Fosters SwissRe-Hochhaus, der Druck auf das Stadtzentrum und die Bereitschaft, diesem nachzugeben, zu erhöhen. Nachdem die Hochhausfrage in Wien lange diskutiert wurde und viele Projekte längst realisiert oder genehmigt waren, beschloss die Stadt Wien 2002 ein Hochhauskonzept. Dieses legt für die Stadt Ausschlusszonen fest, Hochhäuser sind nun grundsätzlich überall möglich außer in diesen. Im einzelnen Fall muss der Bauträger mit einer Reihe von Überprüfungen die Eignung des Standorts nachweisen, etwa bezüglich Verkehrssituation und Beschattung. Während aber gewisse Aspekte mehr oder weniger objektiv darstellbar sind, bleibt doch die Frage, ob sich nicht zwischen dem grundsätzlichen Schutz von Gebieten durch die Ausschlusszonen und der Prüfung des Einzelfalles eine Lücke öffnet, in der Entscheidungen über stadtgestalterisch mehr oder weniger sinnvolle Standorte für Einzeltürme und Cluster zu treffen sind. Doch das wäre dann wohl das Feld der politischen Auseinandersetzung, die durch keine noch so gut fundierte Regel ersetzt werden kann, die aber auch geführt werden muss.

Wien im Verkehrsnetz

Die erste Hälfte der ÖBB-Bahnhofsoffensive ist faktisch abgeschlossen, doch die dringenden Wiener Bahnhofsprojekte sind alle Teil der zweiten Etappe, die gerade erst anläuft. Der Umbau des Bahnhofs Wien Nord durch Albert Wimmer wurde begonnen und wird bis Ende 2007 umgesetzt, ebenso rechtzeitig zur Fußball-Europameisterschaft wie die Verlängerung der U2 über den Praterstern – dann kann auch die neue Oberflächengestaltung von Boris Podrecca realisiert werden. Im Mittelpunkt des Interesses steht natürlich der Bahnhof Wien – Europa Mitte anstelle des heutigen Südbahnhofs, der, wie der Name schon sagt, nicht nur Verkehrsknotenpunkt, sondern auch Symbol für Wiens Integration in einen mittel- und südosteuropäischen Raum sein soll. Dort wird gleichzeitig mit dem Westbahnhof und nach Fertigstellung des Bahnhofs Wien Nord, also 2007, zu bauen begonnen. Der denkmalgeschützte Westbahnhof wird bis 2009 von Heinz Neumann und Eric Steiner umgebaut, wobei alle Bahnhofsfunktionen auf dem Niveau der Gleisanlagen gesammelt werden, während die untere Ebene der Halle mit der nicht mehr benötigten Gepäckmanipulation zur Einkaufsfläche umgewandelt wird. Weiters wird die äußere Mariahilfer Straße mittels einer Passagenebene zwischen der bestehenden Passage von der inneren Mariahilfer Straße und dem Bahnhof besser angebunden und ein neues Gebäude südlich des Bahnhofs errichtet. Die Umsetzung des Gesamtprojektes Westbahnhofareal mit den Bauteilen an der Felberstraße wird dann noch auf sich warten lassen.

Voraussetzung für den geplanten Baubeginn 2007 beim neuen Zentralbahnhof, wenn man nicht bei vollem Betrieb bauen will, ist die temporäre Verlagerung der Süd- und Ostbahnsteige an andere, gut angebundene Orte in der Stadt wie zum Beispiel Meidling und Stadlau. Die den Bahnhof umgebenden Areale können schon vorher in Angriff genommen werden, um einen neuen Stadtteil mit Wohnungen, Büros und Gewerbe zu errichten. Der Bahnhof selbst, der von Albert Wimmer und Theo Hotz/Ernst Hoffmann realisiert werden soll, wäre demnach in zwei Phasen bis 2011 fertig, die jetzige Bahnhofshalle wird

sense for Wien Mitte, one of Vienna's most important transport interchange hubs.

In the European context Vienna is an astonishingly active high-rise city. Other important European cities that place a special emphasis on high-rise buildings include Warsaw and Moscow, where recently a great number of such buildings have been completed, Paris, where the skyscrapers are today confined to La Défense outside the city centre, and Frankfurt with its inner city cluster of bank towers. In London for a long time high-rise buildings were generally erected far outside the centre in Canary Wharf, but ever since Norman Foster's SwissRe Building both pressure on the city centre and willingness to yield to this pressure seem to be growing. After the high-rise question in Vienna had been discussed at length and many projects had been carried out, or had at least had received planning permission, in 2002 the City of Vienna formulated a high-rise concept. This defines zones in the city where high-rise buildings are expressly prohibited, while (in theory) such buildings are permissible everywhere else. In the individual cases the developer must prove the suitability of the location with a series of studies, for instance of the traffic volume created or the amount of shadow cast. While it is possible to present certain aspects in a more or less objective way, the question remains whether a gap might open up between the protection of areas offered by creating prohibited zones on the one hand, and the concept of examining individual cases on the other, in which urban design decisions about the suitability of locations for individual towers or clusters of high-rise buildings could be made. This would most likely become an area for political confrontation of the kind that cannot be replaced by any regulation, no matter how well grounded, but this is a confrontation that must be faced.

Vienna in the Transport Network

The first half of the ÖBB (Austrian Railways) rail offensive is practically complete, but the urgently needed Viennese railway station projects are all part of the second phase, which has only just started. The re-planning of Wien Nord station by Albert Wimmer has begun and construction will be completed by 2007, in time for the European Football Championships, the same applies to the extension of the U2 line to Praterstern (the station serving Wien Nord). Boris Podrecca's new design for the outdoor surfaces at Praterstern can then be carried out. Quite naturally most interest is focussed on the new central railway station, Wien – Europa Mitte (Vienna – Europe Central), which will replace the present Südbahnhof (South Railway Station) and which, as its name implies, will not only be a transport node but also a symbol of Vienna's integration in the central and south-eastern European region. Start of construction for the new central railway station is scheduled for 2007, at the same time as the re-development of the Westbahnhof (West Railway Station) and after completion of Wien Nord. Heinz Neumann and Eric Steiner's redesign of the existing Westbahnhof, which is under a preservation order, will be completed by 2009. All the functions directly relating to railway travel will be combined on the same level as the tracks, whereas the lower level of the hall including the baggage handling area, which is no longer needed, will be converted into retail space. The outer section of Mariahilfer Straße (i.e. beyond the Gürtel) will be better connected by an arcade level between the existing connection from the inner Mariahilfer Straße and the railway station, and a new building will be erected to the south of the existing station. The implementation of the complete project for the Westbahnhof site, including the buildings on Felberstraße, is planned for a later phase.

Henke/Schreieck
Projekt | Development Wien Mitte

abgerissen. Doch damit ist der Bahnhofsinitiative zweiter Teil nicht zu Ende: Der „Schandfleck" Bahnhof Wien Mitte harrt seiner Erneuerung, ein Baubeginn ist vielleicht noch 2005 drin. Und schließlich sollen auch die Bahnhöfe in Heiligenstadt und Hütteldorf erneuert werden, wo durch den denkmalgeschützten Bestand von Otto Wagner enge Rahmen gesetzt sind. Als zentrale Umschlagplätze für Güterbahnverkehr werden Inzersdorf und der Wiener Hafen ausgebaut, sodass die bisher dafür verwendeten Flächen am Süd- und Nordbahnhof anders verwertet werden können – und sehr langfristig trifft das wohl auch auf den Nordwestbahnhof zu. Da aber die Stadtentwicklungsplanung nicht an Wiens Grenzen endet, muss man dieser Liste noch einige weitere Projekte hinzufügen: Der neue Bahnhof Wien – Europa Mitte wird direkt mit dem Flughafen Wien-Schwechat verbunden, sodass Fernzüge am Flughafen halten können und somit dessen Einzugsgebiet radikal vergrößern. Und der CAT, die direkte Bahnanbindung des Flughafens, soll bis zum Flughafen Bratislava weitergeführt werden – der im Übrigen durch wechselseitige Beteiligung mit dem Wiener Flughafen verbunden werden soll, um eine kooperative Entwicklung zu erreichen.

To avoid working on the new central railway station (scheduled start 2007) while the old station is still operational, it is essential to move the platforms for the Südbahn (southern line) and Ostbahn (eastern line) to other well-linked areas of the city, such as Meidling and Stadlau. Work on developing the area around the new railway station could be started earlier to create a new urban district with apartments, offices and commercial space. The railway station building itself, which is to be carried out by Albert Wimmer and Theo Hotz/Ernst Hoffmann would then be completed in two phases by 2011, the present railway station concourse will be demolished. But this is not the end of the second part of the Austrian Rail offensive: the "eyesore" station at Wien Mitte still awaits renovation and re-planning, start of construction in 2005 remains a possibility. And, finally, the railway stations in Heiligenstadt and Hütteldorf are to be renovated. The possibilities here are somewhat restricted due to the fact that the existing buildings by Otto Wagner are under a preservation order. Inzersdorf and the Wiener Hafen (Port of Vienna) are to be developed as central hubs for freight traffic making the existing freight areas at the Nordbahnhof (North Railway Station) and Südbahnhof redundant and therefore available for other functions – in the very long term the same applies to the Nordwestbahnhof (Northwest Railway Station). As the urban development plan does not end at the borders of Vienna, further transport projects can be added to this list. The new railway station Wien – Europa Mitte will be directly connected with Vienna International Airport at Schwechat enabling long-distance trains to stop at the airport and thus radically increasing the

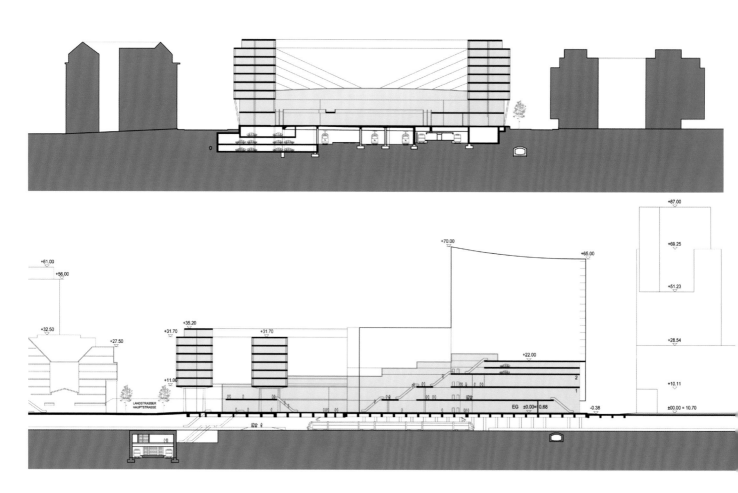

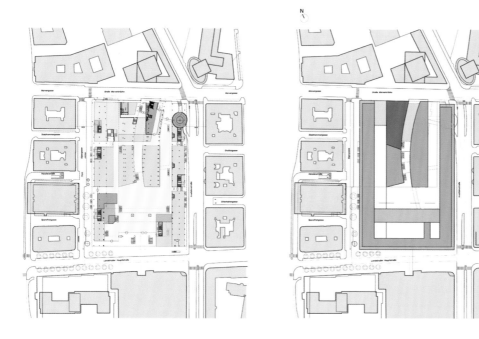

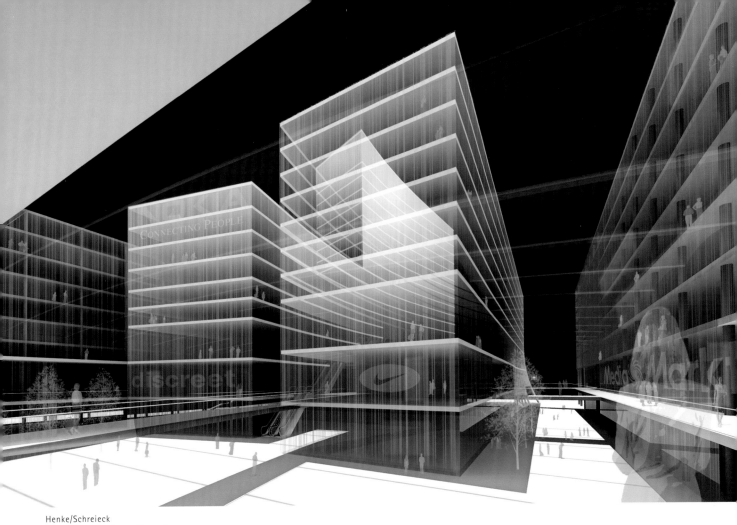

Henke/Schreieck
Wien Mitte: Station, offices, shops

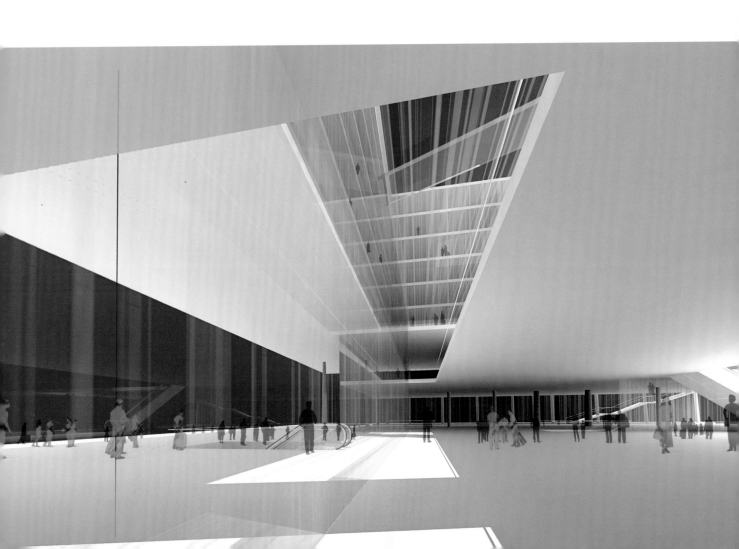

Henke/Schreieck
Wien-Mitte, Detail

Heinz Neumann/Eric Steiner
Projekt Westbahnhof | Western Railway Station development

Wien als Wissensstadt

Die Aktivitäten der Stadt zur Förderung des Standortes für Forschung und für innovative Unternehmen sind vielfältig und reichen von Biotechnologie bis zu den Creative Industries. Der Wissensstandort Wien beschränkt sich aber nicht auf neue, außeruniversitäre Forschungszentren wie das Vienna Biocenter in Erdberg und Wissenschaftsparks wie das Tech Gate Vienna in der Donau-City. Wesentliche Teile dieses Feldes sind auch Bildungseinrichtungen. Größere Baumaßnahmen für Universitäten sind bereits einige Jahre her, so etwa der Neubau für die Veterinärmedizinische Universität und die Umsiedlung der Universität für Musik und darstellende Kunst in den von der Veterinärmedizinischen Universität freigegebenen Bau in der Landstraße. In der jüngeren Vergangenheit wurden eher Adaptionen an den bestehenden Standorten vorgenommen, doch aktuell ist wieder eine Phase der Planung für größere Veränderungen: Die Technische Universität sieht die Umsiedlung größerer Bereiche vor, wofür etwa das Flugfeld Aspern im Gespräch ist, und auch die räumlich äußerst problematische Situation der Wirtschaftsuniversität könnte zu ähnlichen Ideen Anlass geben. Die Universität für angewandte Kunst denkt über eine Übersiedlung in die Donau-City nach, der das sicher gut tun würde, vor allem in der diskutierten Kombination mit einem Haus der Kulturen. Die Frage ist allerdings, wie gut es den inneren Stadtbereichen täte, wenn Universitätsnutzungen mit ihrem Urbanität erzeugenden Umfeld verschwinden, um Raum für Verwaltungs- oder Büroflächen zu schaffen.

Neue Bildungsbauten wurden in Wien durch die Einführung des Fachhochschulstudienmodells Mitte der 1990er Jahre nötig. Derzeit gibt es fünf Anbieter von FH-Studiengängen in Wien mit insgesamt etwa 6.300 Studierenden, das ist ein Viertel aller österreichischen Studienplätze. Während die Fachhochschule des Berufsförderungsinstituts Wien in einem Altbau in der

airport's catchment area, while the CAT, the direct rail connection to Vienna airport, is to be extended to Bratislava airport, the latter is to be linked with Vienna airport by mutual investment in the interest of cooperative development.

Vienna as a City of Knowledge

The activities of the city administration in promoting Vienna as a location for research and innovative businesses are manifold and extend from biotechnology to the so-called creative industries. Vienna as a science location is not confined to the extra-university research centres such as the Vienna Biocenter in Erdberg or science parks such as Tech Gate Vienna in the Donau City, educational and training facilities are also an important part of this field. A number of years ago several large construction projects for the universities were completed, such as the new building for the Veterinary Medicine University and the relocation of the University for Music and the Performing Arts in the old veterinary college building in Landstraße. In the recent past the trend has been more towards adapting existing locations but now the planning of major changes is once again topical: the relocation of larger sections of the University of Technology has been proposed and the airfield at Aspern has been mentioned as a possible location, while the cramped conditions at the Vienna University of Economics and Business Administration could well lead to similar ideas. The University of Applied Arts is considering moving to the Donau City, which would certainly benefit the area, especially if this move were combined with a Haus der Kulturen (House of Cultures), as is being discussed. But there remains the question of the impact on inner city areas when universities, which create a certain type of urbanity in their immediate surroundings, suddenly vanish and make way for administration or office buildings.

Neumann/Steiner
Projekt Westbahnhof | Western Railway Station development

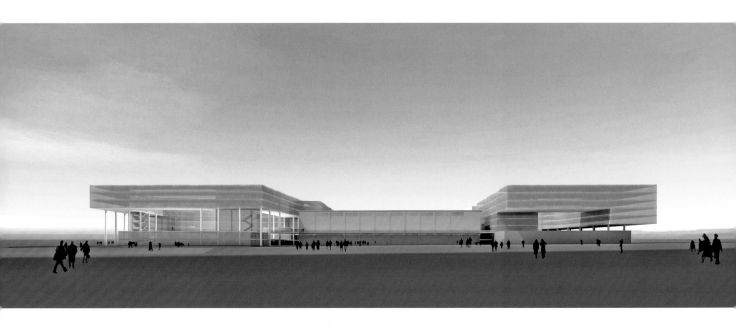

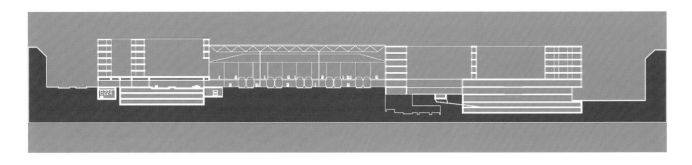

Leopoldstadt untergebracht ist, besitzt die FH Technikum Wien seit zwei Jahren einen Neubau von Elsa Prochazka und Heinz Neumann am Höchstädtplatz, wo sich eine wichtige Entwicklungszone in der Brigittenau befindet. Heuer wurde hier ein neues Gründerzentrum eröffnet, das von der Nähe des Technikums profitieren will, außerdem sind eine Handelschule und Handelsakademie geplant, und Albert Wimmer baut einen 85 Meter hohen Wohnturm. Die FH Campus Wien in Favoriten wird bis 2008 in ein neues Gebäude von Delugan-Meissl am Alten Landgut übersiedeln, wo demnach ebenfalls ein neuer Fokus der Stadtentwicklung ansteht, wenn man die Nähe zu Monte Laa und die geplante Verlängerung der U1 nach Süden bedenkt. Und die FHWien des Wirtschaftsförderungsinstituts wird bis 2007 neben dem WIFI-Gebäude am Währinger Gürtel einen Neubau von Diether Hoppe erhalten. Nicht zu vergessen bleiben jedenfalls die Schulen: Das Wiener Schulbauprogramm 2000 ist Vergangenheit, und seine Neuheit bestand nicht so sehr im Funktionalen, sondern in der Beauftragung einer großen Zahl von renommierten und jungen Architekten. Aktuell wird im Schulbereich offensichtlich nicht an Architektur gedacht, doch es ist klar, dass der vermehrte Einsatz von Nachmittagsbetreuung und Ganztagsschulmodellen auch räumlich Ausdruck finden wird müssen.

In the mid-1990s new buildings for education were required in Vienna as a result of the introduction of the new Fachhochschule (abbr. FH) model, a kind of specialist third-level educational institute. At present five institutions offer this kind of courses in Vienna to around 6,300 students, this is a quarter of the total number of student places in Austria. Whereas the FH of the Berufsförderungsinstitut Wien is housed in an old building in the Leopoldstadt, two years ago the FH Technikum Wien was given a new building designed by Elsa Prochazka and Heinz Neumann on Höchstadtplatz, in an important development zone in the Brigittenau district of Vienna. This year a new "business founders centre" was opened there that is intended to profit from its proximity to the Technikum, a commercial college and commercial academy are planned and Albert Wimmer is building an 85-metre high residential tower. In 2008 the FH Campus Wien in Favoriten will move to a new building designed by Delugan Meissl at Altes Landgut, which, if one considers the closeness to Monte Laa and the planned extension of the U1 line to the south, is also a new focus of urban development. And the FH Wien of the Wirtschaftsförderungsinstitut on Währinger Gürtel will move into a new building by Dieter Hoppe by around 2007. Schools should not be forgotten in this context. The Viennese school building programme 2000 is now history, its novelty lay not so much in the functional area but in the fact that a great number of both famous and young architects were commissioned. At present apparently not much thought is being given to the architecture of schools but it is clear that the growing move towards afternoon supervision of children in schools, and the model of the "all-day school" will at some time have to be given spatial and architectural expression.

Bauprojekte für die Öffentlichkeit:
Prater und Spitäler

Das Messegelände im Wiener Prater entwickelte sich aus der Weltausstellung 1873, deren Gebäude teilweise erhalten blieben und nach dem Ersten Weltkrieg als Messehallen weiter genutzt wurden. Nach dem Zweiten Weltkrieg wurde die Messe wegen des Rotundenbrandes und den Kriegsschäden erneuert. Die Anforderungen der jüngsten Zeit machten nicht mehr nur neue Gebäude, sondern auch eine Flächenreduktion nötig. Nach einer erfolglosen Privatisierung kaufte die Stadt Wien 2000 die Messe zurück und vergab die Betreiberschaft an Reed Exhibitions, um über die Wiener Messe Besitz GmbH Grundstückseigner zu bleiben. Das Gelände wird etwa zur Hälfte weiterhin als Messegelände verwendet, der Rest anderweitig verwertet.

Als Teil eines Masterplans von Heinz Neumann wurden Anfang der 1990er Jahre zwei Hallen errichtet, die nun in das neue Gesamtprojekt integriert sind. Dieses Projekt, bestehend aus einer langgezogenen Mall mit Kopfbau an der Ausstellungsstraße und drei neuen Hallen, die mit Neumanns Halle 25 die neue Messe ergeben, musste in extrem kurzer Zeit zwischen 2000 und 2003 errichtet werden, um rechtzeitig zum Kardiologenkongress fertig zu sein – ein Wettbewerb konnte so schnell nicht durchgeführt werden, war das Argument. Die Generalplanung der Neubauten hatten Fritsch, Chiari und Partner inne, die anfangs mit Norbert Erlach und Gerhard Moßburger als Architekten arbeiteten – diesen wurde dann Gustav Peichl zur Seite gestellt, der schließlich einen großen Teil der Gestaltung bestimmte. 2005 folgte das Messehotel von Hermann Czech, sodass die Messeinfrastruktur jetzt bis auf die Anbindung an die neue U-Bahnlinie fertig gestellt ist.

Die Flächen südlich der Nordportalstraße, also zum Volksprater und zum Grünen Prater hin, stehen somit für andere Nutzungen zur Verfügung, sie sollen teils dem Wurstelprater zugeschlagen werden, die restliche, größere Fläche wird bereits jetzt als Veranstaltungsplatz genützt und soll auch langfristig der Unterhaltung gewidmet bleiben. Die städtebauliche Planung für dieses Areal wird erst begonnen. Schließlich bleibt noch ein kleineres Grundstück, das jetzt von der U-Bahnbaustelle genützt wird und nordöstlich der neuen U-Bahntrasse liegt – die dortige Nutzung ist noch unklar, wird aber wohl in Abstimmung mit der Fläche der gegenüberliegenden Albrechtskaserne entwickelt, wo ein Technologiepark geplant ist. Weitere in der Nähe liegende und zu entwickelnde Gebiete entlang der U2, die 2008 fertig sein wird, befinden sich zwischen Krieau und Vorgartenstraße, zwischen den beiden Stadien, in der Wilhelmskaserne und bei der Praterbrücke – und auch das weitere Schicksal der Trabrenngründe ist ungewiss. Es bleibt also genügend Potenzial für mehrere Jahrzehnte. Eines der ersten Projekte für das Gebiet ist ein Einkaufszentrum am Olympiaplatz, beim Ernst-Happel-Stadion, das noch heuer begonnen werden soll – angesichts der enormen Liste an geplanten Shoppingflächen in Wien und der dauernden Sorge um Wiens Einkaufsstraßen ein diskussionswürdiges Vorhaben.

Lage und Angebotsspektrum der Wiener Spitäler müssen sich ändernden Erfordernissen der Bevölkerungsverteilung angepasst werden – wegen der wachsender Bewohnerzahlen werden in Zukunft Spitalskapazitäten vom Westen in den Nordosten verlagert, so ist etwa das Heeresspital in Stammersdorf potenzieller Ort für ein neues Krankenhaus. Gleichzeitig altert die Wiener Bevölkerung, sodass ein Mehrbedarf an Pflegeeinrichtungen besteht. Schon bisher gab es Verlagerungen aus ökonomischen und organisatorischen Gründen. Beispielhaft für diese Entwicklung steht das nunmehr Otto-Wagner-Spital genannte Ensemble auf der Baumgartner Höhe. Dort befanden sich bis vor kurzem vier verschiedene Einrichtungen (Psychiatrie, Pulmologie, Pflegeheim und Förderpflegeheim), die

Building Projects for the Public:
Prater and Hospitals

The Messegelände (trade fair grounds) in the Prater developed from the World Exhibition held there in 1873, some of the original buildings were preserved and continued to be used for fairs after the First World War. Following the Second World War the Fair had to be completely renovated on account of a major fire that destroyed the Rotunda and the damage caused by wartime bombing. More recently new demands made not only new buildings but also a reduction in the total floor area necessary. After an unsuccessful privatisation the City of Vienna reacquired the Messe and handed over the running of trade fairs to Reed Exhibitions while remaining owner of the site through the Wiener Messe Besitz GmbH. About half of the site will continue to be used for fairs while different functions will be found for the remainder.

As part of a master plan by Heinz Neumann at the start of the 1990s, two new halls were erected which have now been integrated in the new overall project. This project consists of an elongated mall with an end building on Ausstellungstraße and three new halls which, together with Neumann's hall 25 constitute the new Wiener Messe (Vienna Fair). The complex had to be erected in a very short period between 2000 and 2003 to be ready in time for a major cardiologists conference – it was argued that it was not feasible to hold a competition in this short space of time. The general planners for the new buildings were Fritsch, Chiari und Partner, who initially worked with Norbert Erlach and Gerhard Moßburger as architects. Gustav Peichl then joined the constellation and ultimately decided a large part of the design. In 2005 the trade fair hotel by Hermann Czech followed so that, apart from the new connection to the Underground network, the infrastructure is now complete.

The areas to the south of Nordportalstraße, i.e. towards the Volksprater and the Grüner Prater, are now available for other functions. Part will be allotted to the so-called Wurstelprater (fun-fair), the larger remaining part of the site is already being used as an events space and the long-term plan is that it should continue to serve as an entertainment area. Urban planning for this part of the city has only just begun. Finally, there still remains a small site, presently part of the building site for the extension to the Underground, which lies to the northeast of the new Underground line. The future use for this area is yet to be clarified but will most likely be decided in conjunction with the proposals for the Albrechtskaserne (barracks) opposite, where a technology park is planned. Further areas to be developed along the extended U2 line, which is scheduled for completion in 2008, are located between Krieau and Vorgartenstraße, between the two stadiums, in the Wilhelmskaserne (barracks) and near Praterbrücke (bridge), the future of the Trabrenngründe (trotting race course) also remains uncertain. Thus there is certainly enough potential for several decades. One of the first projects for this area is a shopping centre at Olympiaplatz, near Ernst Happel Stadium, construction is scheduled to start this year. Given the enormous amount of planned retail space in Vienna and the repeatedly voiced worries about the future of Vienna's established shopping streets this project certainly provides fuel for discussion.

The location of and the range of facilities offered by Vienna's hospitals will have to be adapted to meet the changing needs of the different sections of the population. Due to local increases in population in the future the concentration of hospital facilities will be shifted from the west to the northeast, the military hospital in Stammersdorf, for example, is a possible location for a new hospital. At the same time the ageing population of Vienna means that there is an increased need

Franz Kuzmich/MA21/WES & Partner
Viertel Zwei Development, Wien-Prater
RENDERING IC PROJEKTENTWICKLUNG

nach dem Umzug des Neurologischen Zentrums aus Döbling an diesem Standort zu einem einzigen Spital mit Pflegezentrum zusammengefasst wurden. Die organisatorische und bauliche Entwicklung ist im Rahmen eines so genannten Zielplans von Norbert Erlach organisiert, der ab 1997 zehn Jahre lang läuft und alle Veränderungen aufgrund des Bedarfs für diesen Zeitraum plant, inklusive der räumlichen Adaptierungen. Teil dieser Entwicklung war auch der Umbau einiger Pavillons, beispielsweise der drei neurologischen durch Ernst Beneder und Anja Fischer, eines geriatrischen durch Alexander Runser und Christa Prantl und eines psychiatrischen durch August Sarnitz und Soyka/Silber/Soyka. Bis zum 100. Jubiläum der Anlage von Otto Wagner im Jahr 2007 soll die Anstaltskirche generalsaniert sein. Weitere Maßnahmen sind geplant, aber aus budgetären Gründen auf Eis gelegt – es bleibt zu hoffen, dass die bauliche Entwicklung dieses Ensembles auf gleichem Niveau weitergeführt wird. Ein ähnlicher Zielplan, ebenfalls von Norbert Erlach erstellt, lag der Entwicklung des Kaiser-Franz-Josef-Spitals in Favoriten zum Sozialmedizinischen Zentrum Süd zugrunde, das neben dem Krankenhaus aus einem von Anton Schweighofer geplanten Geriatriezentrum besteht.

for care facilities for the elderly. Changes in the concentration and location of medical facilities have already been made due to economic and organisational reasons. One example of this development is the Baumgartner Höhe complex, now known as the Otto Wagner Spital. Until recently this complex consisted of four separate facilities (psychiatry, pneumology, nursing home and therapeutic care centre) which, following the move of the neurological centre from Döbling to the Otto Wagner Spital, were combined to form a single hospital with nursing home. The organisational and constructional development is organised within the framework of a so-called "target plan" formulated by Norbert Erlach, which was started in 1997 and runs for ten years and plans all the necessary changes (including adaptations to buildings). Part of this development was the re-planning of a number of the existing pavilions, for example three neurological pavilions were re-planned by architects Ernst Beneder and Anja Fischer, a geriatric pavilion was redesigned by Alexander Runser and Christa Prantl and one of the psychiatric pavilions by August Sarnitz and Soyka/Silber/Soyka. By the 100th anniversary of the Otto Wagner complex (in 2007) Wagner's famous Jugendstil church will have been completely renovated. Further measures are planned but have been put on hold for cost reasons – it is to be hoped that the architectural development of this ensemble will be continued at the same high level. A similar target plan, also conceived by Norbert Erlach, formed the basis for the development of the Kaiser-Franz-Josef-Spital in Favoriten into the Sozialmedizinisches Zentrum Süd, which, in addition to the hospital, includes a geriatric medicine centre designed by Anton Schweighofer.

Peichl & Partner; Erlach & Moßburger; Fritsch, Chiari & Partner
Messe Wien | Vienna Fair
PHOTOS ANNA BLAU

Hermann Czech
Hotel Messe Wien
PHOTOS ANNA BLAU

Die Entwicklung der historischen Stadt

Das Verhältnis der Wiener Stadtverwaltung zur gründerzeitlichen Bausubstanz Wiens war seit der Gründung der Republik immer ein schwieriges, was angesichts der Wohnverhältnisse in diesen Vierteln zur damaligen Zeit kein Wunder ist. Der Wohnbau des Roten Wien integrierte sich einerseits häufig in die gründerzeitliche Stadtstruktur, setzte sich aber andererseits von Prinzipien des gründerzeitlichen Wohnbaus deutlich ab. Heute hat der gründerzeitliche Wohnbestand eine deutliche Wandlung durchgemacht, auch wenn es natürlich nach wie vor Gebiete und Bauten mit sehr ungenügenden Wohnverhältnissen gibt. Etwa ein Viertel der Wiener Wohnungen befindet sich in gründerzeitlichen Häusern, von denen viele stark verändert wurden: Wohnungszusammenlegungen, Ausbau mit heutigen sanitären Standards, Erdgeschoß- und Wohnungsumnutzungen, Garageneinbauten, Hofentkernungen, Aufstockungen und Dachausbauten, aber auch das lange Zeit übliche Abschlagen der Fassadenornamentik. Teil einer Wandlung zum Positiven war sicherlich der Anfang der 1970er Jahre begonnene Paradigmenwechsel hin zum Wiener Modell der „sanften Stadterneuerung". Im STEP 05 (siehe S. 32) wird die gründerzeitliche Stadt erstmals nicht nur als Feld der Wohnbausanierung, sondern auch als Ort eines wirtschaftlichen Sektors mit eigenen Möglichkeiten dargestellt. Dabei handelt es sich etwa um Kleinteiligkeit, Nähe von Wohnen und Arbeiten, enge Vernetzungsmöglichkeiten, Urbanität und lokale Orientierung. Aspekte dieser Wirtschaft der gründerzeitlichen Stadt sind die Einkaufsstraßen und die Büronutzung durch KMUs, bei denen es sich besonders um Dienstleistungen im wirtschaftlich-rechtlichen Bereich, um die Gesundheitsbranche und um die viel zitierten Creative Industries handelt, die geradezu als Erneuerungspotenzial für sterbende Einkaufsstraßen gesehen werden, indem etwa Architekturbüros Erdgeschoßlokale als Standort übernehmen. Das Potenzial ist groß, und es bleibt zu hoffen, dass die

The Development of the Historic City

Ever since founding of the Austrian Republic, the relationship of Vienna's municipal administration to the city's 19th century built fabric has been a difficult one, which, given the living conditions that once existed in these areas, is hardly surprising. While the housing projects of "Red Vienna" are often integrated in the 19th century urban structure they differ essentially from the principles of 19th century housing. Today the 19th century housing stock has undergone a clear change although there still remain areas and buildings with unsatisfactory living conditions. About one quarter of the dwellings in Vienna are in 19th century buildings, many of which have been radically altered: on the positive side apartments have been combined and equipped to meet modern standards, ground floor zones and a number of dwellings have found new uses, garages have been built, courtyards cleared of unused or unseemly buildings, storeys added and attics converted, on the negative side for a long time it was standard practice to remove the façade ornament from 19th century tenement blocks. An element in the move to a more positive approach was certainly a change of paradigms at the beginning of the 1970s leading to the Viennese model of "gentle urban renewal". In STEP 05 (see p. 32) the 19th century city is, for the first time, presented not only as an area where the housing stock must be refurbished but also as the location of an economic sector with its own possibilities. These include the small-scale composition of these parts of the city, the proximity of housing and workplace, good transport connections, urbanity and the neighbourhood quality. Aspects of the economy of the 19th century city include the shopping streets and the offices of small and medium-sized businesses – often service industries in the commercial law sector, health sector businesses or the often-cited creative industries that are seen as a potent source of new life for dying shopping streets. One

Henke/Schreieck
k 47 – Downtown office building
PHOTOS ANNA BLAU

politische Sensibilität im Hinblick auf das Wohnen in Wien ausgeprägt genug ist, um negative Gentrifizierungseffekte zu verhindern.

Beispielhaft für den Umgang mit abgewerteten Gründerzeitvierteln sind die Projekte im Bereich des westlichen Gürtels, einerseits die EU-Förderung im Rahmen des URBAN-Programms und andererseits das von privater Seite gestartete Kunstprojekt SOHO in Ottakring. Im Rahmen des EU-Programms sollte von 1995 bis 2000 ein massiver Impuls für die verödeten Areale des Westgürtels gesetzt werden. Die Planung umfasste Maßnahmen der sanften Stadterneuerung und die Gemeindebau-Sanierung, am sichtbarsten war aber die Aufwertung des Gürtels selbst, indem das Potenzial der Stadtbahnbögen von Otto Wagner genützt wurde. In Silja Tillners URBION-Projekt sanierte man die Vorbereiche zu beiden Seiten des Viaduktes und verwandelte die Räume unter den Bögen durch Glasfassaden in ideale Orte für Lokale. Projekte wie die Hauptbücherei und die Neuerrichtung von Bürobauten am Gürtel trugen das ihre bei. Am wichtigsten ist aber wohl, dass die Initiative nicht mit dem Auslaufen der EU-Förderung endet, sondern fortgesetzt wird. Ein zukünftiger Fokus wird der Gaudenzdorfer Knoten sein, für den ein groß angelegter Ideenfindungsprozess geplant ist.

Seit 1999 findet jährlich SOHO in Ottakring statt, initiiert von der Künstlerin Ula Schneider. Mit Unterstützung der Stadt und der Wirtschaftskammer wurde jedes Jahr am Anfang des Sommers das Brunnenviertel für zwei Wochen zum Kunstort, indem leere ebenso wie genützte Lokale und der öffentliche Raum für Präsentationen verwendet wurden. Das Projekt trug nach und

example here is the architects practices that have recently occupied what were once ground floor shops. The potential is sizable and it remains to be hoped that political awareness of Vienna as a city to live in is sufficiently developed to hinder any possible negative effects of gentrification.

Positive examples of the treatment of run-down 19th century areas include projects for the western part of the Gürtel: on the one hand the EU grants provided in the framework of the URBAN programme, on the other the private initiative of the SOHO art project in Ottakring. Within the context of the EU programme between 1995 and 2000 a massive initiative was started to rescue the decaying areas of the West Gürtel. The planning included measures of "gentle urban renewal" and the renovation of social housing, however the most visible aspect was the improvement of the Gürtel itself through exploiting the potential offered by the arches of Otto Wagner's viaduct that carries the U6 railway line. In Silja Tillner's URBION project the areas on either side of the viaduct were renovated and through the use of completely glazed facades the spaces under the arches were transformed into ideal locations for bars and restaurants. Projects such as the Hauptbücherei (Main City Library) and the new office buildings along the Gürtel also made important contributions to reviving the area. But probably the most important thing is that the initiative should be continued when the EU funds cease to flow. A focal point in the future will be the Gaudenzdorfer Knoten where it is planned to launch a large-scale initiative to discover ideas. Since 1999 SOHO, initiated by the artist Ula Schneider, has been held annually in Ottakring. With the support of the city

Richard & Karin Zeitlhuber
Ilgplatz, Leopoldstadt
PHOTO ANNA BLAU

nach zu einer Aufwertung bei, leer stehende Geschäftslokale fanden neue Nutzer, sodass es schließlich einerseits zu Vereinnahmungsversuchen und andererseits zu Vorwürfen an SOHO kam, die Gentrifizierung zu fördern. Nach einer grundsätzlichen Konzeptadaptierung 2004 ist der Rhythmus nun zweijährlich, und die inhaltliche Orientierung ist wesentlich fokussierter auf Kunst im öffentlichen Raum, Partizipation und emanzipatorische Strategien für die Bewohner des Viertels ausgerichtet. Gerade dieses Projekt, das von Anfang an auf die Einbeziehung von Migranten setzte, macht deutlich, dass Stadterneuerung nicht nur mit materieller Substanz zu tun hat, und so plant Wien laut STEP 05, beim Zielgebiet Gürtel dezidiert auf Diversitätspolitik zu setzen. Schließlich ist das SOHO-Gebiet auch Ort eines Projektes zur Verbesserung des öffentlichen Raumes mit Bewohnerbeteiligung: Ernst Mateovics und Brigitta Maczek realisierten dort bis 2000 zusammen mit KoseLička die Neugestaltung des Yppenplatzes, nach einer längeren Pause, die unter anderem für die Beteiligung der Betroffenen genützt wurde, beginnt heuer die Erneuerung des Brunnenmarktes, der nun in eine Fußgängerzone umgewandelt und besser mit dem Umfeld verbunden werden soll.

Es gibt allerdings auch Gründerzeitviertel, in denen eine andere Form von Stadtentwicklung im Mittelpunkt steht, nämlich der Dachausbau. In den vergangenen Jahren wurden immer mehr und immer größere Aufbauten realisiert, die Auseinandersetzung um den Weltkulturerbestatus Wiens hat zu einer breiten Diskussion dieser Entwicklung geführt, sodass die Stadt die großen Gestaltungsfreiheiten, die sich aus der Bauordnungsnovelle 1996 ergaben, nunmehr ein wenig einschränkt. Ein formal

and the chamber of commerce every year at the beginning of summer, the area around the Brunnengasse market was transformed for two weeks into a kind of art centre by using empty and functioning shops as well as public space for presentations. The project contributed to a gradual improvement of the area and empty ground floor premises found new users, so that, on the one hand, attempts were made to take over this initiative, while on the other SOHO was accused of promoting the process of gentrification. After a fundamental rethinking of the concept in 2004 the rhythm is now biannual and the focus is more on art in public space, participation and emancipational strategies for the residents of the area. Precisely this project that, from the very start, counted on the involvement of the local immigrant population, makes it very clear that urban renewal does not deal with material substance alone, therefore in STEP 05 Vienna plans to place a clear emphasis on a policy of diversity in the Gürtel target area. Finally, the SOHO area is also the location of a project aimed at improving public space with the involvement of local residents: up to 2000 Ernst Mateovics and Brigitta Maczek together with KoseLička carried out the re-design of Yppenplatz; following a longer pause (which was also exploited to secure the involvement of those directly affected) this year a start will be made with the renewal of the Brunnen market, which is to be transformed into a pedestrian zone and better connected with the surrounding area.

There are, however, also 19th century districts where a different kind of urban development, namely the attic conversion, is the main focus. In recent years more and more roof top ad-

außergewöhnliches, doch in seiner Dimension mit bis zu drei Geschoßen typisches Projekt ist der Dachausbau des Hanuschhofs zwischen Albertina und Burggarten mit Luxuswohnungen in spektakulären Formen durch Silberpfeil Architekten. Beispiellos ist der Dachausbau Ray 1 von Delugan-Meissl, der zwar auf einem Bürogebäude der 60er Jahre, aber im gründerzeitlichen Kontext des Bezirks Margareten realisiert wurde und Möglichkeiten aufzeigt, die jenseits der maximalen Ausnützung liegen.

Nicht nur die Bauten der Gründerzeit, auch ihre öffentlichen Räume erfuhren im Laufe des vergangenen Jahrhunderts Veränderungen, insbesondere durch den Autoverkehr. Während der Schwarzenbergplatz in der Vergangenheit Flaniermeile, Wohnort der Hocharistokratie und symbolischer Ort des Heeres war, ist er nun vor allem Verkehrsknotenpunkt. Eine dem entsprechende Umgestaltung durch Alfredo Arribas konzentrierte sich auf die Beleuchtung und kann dem Fußgänger hauptsächlich die Möglichkeit der schnellen Querung bieten. Dem gegenüber steht das Projekt von Richard und Karin Zeitlhuber für den kleinen Ilgplatz in der Leopoldstadt, der für die Fußgänger und Außenraumbenützer zurückgewonnen werden konnte. Großräumigere Bedeutung besitzen die ehemaligen Ländeanlagen des Donaukanals, die auch seit einiger Zeit im Mittelpunkt der Aufmerksamkeit stehen. Größere Bauprojekte der vergangenen Jahre in ihrem Umfeld, ob nun Wasser- oder U-Bahnbau, erhöhten die Notwendigkeit einer Neukonzeption, und nun sind vielfältige Ideen von der Errichtung einer bebauten Brücke ähnlich der Florentiner Ponte Vecchio bis zu Badeanlagen am Tisch. Am wichtigsten sind beim Donaukanal aber wohl nicht neue Strukturen, sondern eine behutsame Grundausstattung mit Zugängen, Beleuchtung und sanitären Anlagen.

ditions have been built and the discussion on Vienna's status as part of the UNESCO world cultural heritage lead to such a wide-ranging debate about this phenomenon that the authorities have recently somewhat restricted the design freedom in this area that had resulted from an amendment to the building regulations passed in 1996. A project that in formal terms is rather unusual but which, in terms of dimensions, (the attic conversion is up to three storeys in height) is typical of this trend, is the rooftop development of the Hanuschhof, between the Albertina and the Burggarten, where luxury apartments are housed in a spectacularly shaped shell designed by Silberpfeil Architekten. The attic conversion Ray 1 by Delugan Meissl that, although built on top of a 1960s office building, lies in the predominantly 19th century district of Margareten is exceptional and demonstrates possibilities that go much further than the exploitation of the available space.

Not only the 19th century buildings but also the public spaces from this period have experienced considerable changes in the course of the last century, in particular due motorised traffic. Whereas once Schwarzenbergplatz was an area with a symbolic meaning for the military, where the citizens strolled and the aristocracy lived, today it is, above all, a major traffic intersection. Alfredo Arribas redesign reflected this situation and concentrated on the lighting and, primarily, allows pedestrians to cross the square more easily and safely. A contrast to this design is offered by Richard and Karin Zeitlhuber's project for the little Ilgplatz in the Leopoldstadt, where it proved possible to regain space for pedestrians and those who use outdoor space. The former landing stages along the Danube Canal have a greater urban impact and have been a focus of attention for a number of years. In recent years large construction projects in the surrounding area, whether for the water system or the underground railway, have increased the need for a new concept, today diverse ideas ranging from the construction of a bridge with buildings on it, like the Ponte Vecchio in Florence, to bathing facilities are the subject of discussion. However, the most important thing for the Danube Canal is not new structures but rather a careful equipping of the area with proper approaches, lighting and sanitary facilities.

PHOTO MA 13, MEDIA WIEN

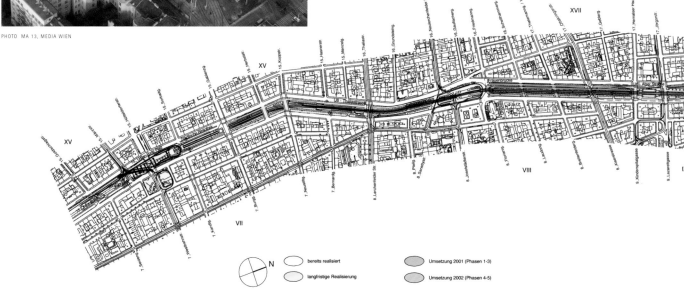

Silja Tillner et alia
Urban Intervention Gürtel West

PHOTOS ANNA BLAU

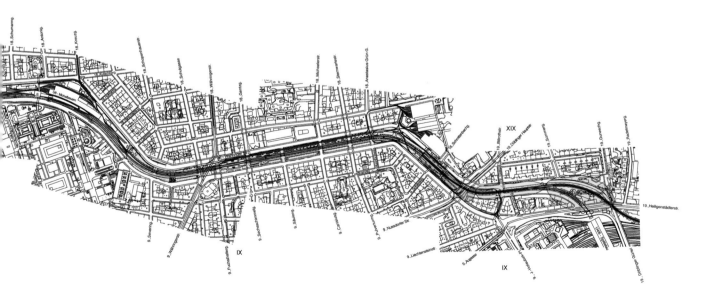

Stadtentwicklung Wien heute

Man kann bei der Betrachtung von Wiens Stadtentwicklung ohne Zweifel feststellen, dass die Stadtregierung das Ziel einer bewohnerorientierten, hochwertigen Entwicklung anstrebt. Dem gegenüber stehen die heute wesentlich beschränkteren Möglichkeiten der politischen Planung. Der neue Ansatz des STEP 05, neben einer regelmäßigen Zusammenschau wichtiger Themen und Planungen auch eine Zielkontrolle darüber einzuführen, ist sicherlich ein Schritt in die richtige Richtung. Trotz dieser Situation bleibt jedoch unbegreiflich, warum wichtige Infrastrukturprojekte des öffentlichen Verkehrs wie der symbolisch hoch aufgeladene Bahnhof Wien - Europa Mitte erst fast zwanzig Jahre nach der Wende in Ostmitteleuropa begonnen werden können, und wie mit den stadtplanungspolitischen Zielen unvereinbare Projekte wie Wienerberg und Monte Laa realisiert werden konnten.

Wichtig wird jedenfalls die Politik im Hinblick auf eine Weiterentwicklung der „Wissensstadt" Wien sein, von den Creative Industries über Schulen und Universitäten bis zu Forschungseinrichtungen – ein Thema, bei dem Bauliches sicherlich nicht

Vienna's Urban Development Today

A look at Vienna's urban development allows the assertion that the municipal authorities pursue a goal of resident-oriented, high quality development. This goal must be seen in the light of the opportunities currently available to political planning, which are far more restricted than previously. The new approach taken in STEP 05, the introduction of an assessment of planning goals in addition to the regular compilation of important themes and plans, is certainly a step in the right direction. Despite this improved situation it remains incomprehensible that important infrastructure projects for the public transport system, such as the symbolic and highly emotionally charged railway station Wien - Europa Mitte, were started only almost twenty years after the political changes in eastern central Europe. It is equally difficult to understand how projects such as Monte Laa and Wienerberg, which are completely at odds with the goals of urban planning policy, could be carried out in the first place.

Politics will certainly grow in importance in Vienna's future development as a "city of knowledge", from the creative

im Mittelpunkt steht, aber zusammen mit Standortfragen durchaus Bedeutung besitzt. Es ist auch klar, dass – wie es ja im aktuellen STEP 05 anklingt – eine weitergehende Auseinandersetzung mit dem Bestand, der gründerzeitlichen Stadt, aber auch mit dem Bestand aus dem 20. Jahrhundert, etwa den Projekten der äußeren Stadterweiterung, von großer Bedeutung ist. Wien ist einerseits eine Stadt, die in vielerlei Hinsicht von historischer Architektur und Städtebau lebt, andererseits aber in gewissen Bereichen bauliche Innovationen zuließ, man denke an den Wohnbau oder die Hochhausfrage, in der Wien freizügiger ist als die meisten europäischen Städte. Eine Kombination dieser Faktoren, das „Weiterbauen" am Bestand und die Integration des Neuen, hat jedenfalls Zukunftspotenzial. Projekte wie die Gürtelentwicklung zeigen, dass dabei nicht allein die materielle Substanz im Fokus steht, diese aber wesentliche Bedeutung hat. Ein neuerlicher Innovationsschub, etwa in der Wohnbaufrage, wäre jedenfalls wünschenswert.

industries to the schools, universities and research facilities – a theme where buildings, while they will not occupy the centre point will still remain of great importance (as indeed will the question of location). It is also clear that – as implied in the current STEP 05 – a further examination of the existing substance (both the 19th century city and also the 20th century fabric, e.g. the "outer" urban development projects) is of major importance. Vienna is, on the one hand, a city that in many respects lives from its historic architecture and urban planning but that, on the other hand, has also permitted innovative building in certain areas, one thinks here of housing or the high-rise building question, where Vienna takes a considerably more liberal stance than most European cities. A combination of these two factors, the "further development" of the existing fabric and the integration of the new, certainly offers potential for the future. Projects such as the Gürtel development show that, while the material substance alone does not form the focus, it nevertheless retains an important significance. A new phase of innovation, for instance in the housing question, is certainly desirable.

Architektur Consult

www.archconsult.com

Günther Domenig

www.domenig.at
geboren | born 1934 in Klagenfurt
Studium | education TU Graz (Diplom | graduated
in 1959)
Büro | studio seit | since 1973 in Graz, Klagenfurt
und Wien
Lehrtätigkeit | teaching 1980-2000 Professor TU
Graz

Im Springer Verlag erschien 2005 die Monographie | published by Springer in 2005: „Günther
Domenig: Recent Work" (German | English edition)

Hermann Eisenköck

www.eisenkoeck.com
geboren | born 1954 in Salzburg
Studium | education TU Graz (Diplom | graduated
in 1981)
Partnerschaft | collaboration seit | since 1986
mit | with Günther Domenig
Büro | studio seit 1998 gemeinsam mit Herfried
Peyker geschäftsführender Partner der Architektur
Consult ZT | since 1998 managing partner of Architektur Consult with Herfried Pyker

Herfried Peyker

www.archconsult.com
geboren | born 1947 in Kärnten
Studium | education TU Graz (Diplom | graduated
in 1975)
Partnerschaft | collaboration Werkgruppe Graz
und/and Gruppe 3 (mit | with Werner Nussmüller,
Nikolaus Schuster)

Werke | projects
T-Center Wien; max mobile Call Center, Graz;
Heidenbauer Metallbau in Bruck a.d.Mur; AHS
Wolkersdorf; Kulturhalle | cultural center Lannach;
Druckerei Carnthia | Carinthia printing plant;
Mehrzweckhalle und Sicherheitszentrum, Velden
| Velden multi purpose hall and security center;
Stadion St. Veit | St. Veit stadium

BEHF

www.behf.at

Partner | partners Armin Ebner, Susi Hasenauer,
Stephan Ferenczy
Studium | education Universität für angewandte
Kunst in Wien | University of Applied Arts, Vienna
Büro | studio seit | since 1995 in Wien | Vienna

Werke | projects
Libromania-Stores; Footsteps-Shops, Stiefelkönig-
Stores; Shopping Center Feldbach; C&A-City Linz;
Geschäftshaus | office building Koschatstraße,
Büro | office Rutter in Klagenfurt; Halle Rigler in
Waidhofen/Ybbs; Restaurants Fabios, Yume, Yellow,
Mr. Lee 1 & 2 Wien | Vienna; Umbau | conversion
Volkskundemuseum in Graz; MQ 21/Erste Bank
Arena Wien | Vienna

Luigi Blau

www.luigiblau.at

geboren | born 1945
Studium | education Akademie der bildenden
Künste in Wien, Meisterklasse Ernst A. Plischke
(Diplom 1973) | Academy of Fine Arts Vienna
under Ernst A. Plischke (graduated in 1973)

Werke | projects
Zahlreiche Geschäftsumbauten und Einrichtungen
| numerous shop designs; Einfamilienhäuser wie
das Haus Bene in Waidhofen/Ybbs und das Haus
Wittmann/Hofer in Etsdorf | single family houses:
Bene House in Waidhofen/Ybbs, Wittmann/Hofer
House in Etsdorf; Umbau des Wiener Ronacher Theaters | conversion of the Ronacher Theater Vienna;
Gestaltung des Theatercafés im Wiener Burgtheater
| Theatercafé Vienna Burgtheater

Im Springer Verlag erschien 2003 die Monographie
| published by Springer in 2003: „Architekt Luigi
Blau. Häuser, Interieurs, Stadtmöbel. Beiträge zur
Baukultur 1967-2002"

EOOS

www.eoos.com

Partner | partners Martin Bergmann, Gernot
Bohmann, Harald Gründl
Studium | education Universität für angewandte
Kunst, Wien | University of Applied Arts Vienna
Büro | studio seit 1995 in Wien | Vienna; tätig in
den Bereichen | working fields furniture | product,
flagship store | brand zone, research

Werke | projects
Giorgio Armani Cosmetics – World Wide Shop
Concept; adidas „Originals" – World Wide Shop
Concept; A1 Lounge Vienna; Möbel und Produkt-
design für | furniture and product designs for
Walter Knoll, Moroso, Matteograssi, Keilhauer,
Duravit, artelano, Montina, Red Bull, Alessi, Abet
Laminati, Zumtobel Staff

Falkeis & Falkeis-Senn Architekten

www.falkeis-architekten.at

Partner | partners Anton Falkeis, Cornelia Falkeis-
Senn
Studium | education Universität für angewandte
Kunst, Wien | University of Applied Arts Vienna
(Diplom | graduated in 1986)
Lehrtätigkeit | teaching
Anton Falkeis: Universität für angewandte Kunst,
Wien | University of Applied Arts Vienna, University
of Tokyo (Research)
Cornelia Falkeis-Senn: TU Wien | Vienna, University
of Tokyo (Research)

Werke | projects
Bank und Gemeindeamt Prutz | bank branch and
community center Prutz; Haus der Musik in Tirol;
Dachgeschoßausbauten in Wien | roof top exten-
sions in Vienna; Einfamilienhäuser | single family
houses

Boris Podrecca

geboren | born 1941
Studium | education TU Wien und an der Akademie
der bildenden Künste in Wien (Diplom 1968) |
Vienna TU and Academy of Fine Arts Vienna (gra-
duated in 1968)
Lehrtätigkeit | teaching seit 1988 Professor für
Raumgestaltung und Entwerfen an der TU Stuttgart
| since 1988 Professor at Stuttgart TU

Werke | projects
Umbauten historischer Bausubstanz und Neugestaltung historischer Plätze etwa in Piran, Cormons, Bologna, Venedig, Verona und in Österreich
| conversions and redesign of historic squares in
Piran, Cormons, Bologna, Venice, Verona and in
Austria; Millenniums Tower (mit | with G.Peichl
& R.F.Weber, 1999), Um- und Zubau Universi-
tät Maribor | extension University of Marobor,
Hotel Greif Bozen | Bolzano; City Kaufhaus Steyr
| department store in Steyr; Weingut Bric | Bric
winery; Wohnpark Hetzendorf | Hetzendorf housing
complex; Vienna Biocenter; Hotel Mons, Ljubljana

Im Springer Verlag erschien 2004: „Boris Podrecca:
Offene Räume" | published by Springer in 2004:
„Boris Podrecca: Public Spaces" (German | English
edition)

RATAPLAN
www.rataplan.at

Partner | partners Rudi Fritz, Susanne Höhndorf,
Gerhard Huber, Martina Schöberl, Friedel Winkler
Studium | education in Wien, Berlin und Stuttgart |
in Vienna, Berlin and Stuttgart
Büro | studio Zusammenarbeit seit 1989 | collabo-
ration since 1989
1993 Gründung von RATAPLAN | founded RATA-
PLAN in 1993

Werke | projects
Zahlreiche Wohnungs-, Büroumbauten und Dach-
geschoßausbauten in Wien | numerous apartment,
office and roof top conversions in Vienna; Villa de
Campos in Niger/West Africa; Ferienhaus | vacation
home in Baldramsdorf; zwei Geschoßwohnbauten
in Wien | two multi-story housing complexes in
Vienna; Stadtvillen Wien | City Villas Vienna

schluderarchitektur
www.architecture.at

Michael Schluder
geboren | born 1956 in Wien/Vienna
Studium | education TU Wien/Vienna (Diplom |
graduated in 1986)
Büro | studio 1988-2002 schluder/kastner
seit | since 2002 schluderarchitektur

Werke | projects
Wohnbauten und Dachgeschoßausbauten in Wien
| housing complexes and roof top extensions in
Vienna; Büro-Neubauten und Umbauten | office
buildings and conversions; Konzeptplanung und
Ausführung von Gastronomie- und Hotelumbauten
| concept and planning of restaurants and hotel
conversions (Wein&Co, Gartenhotel Altmannsdorf);
Produktentwicklung von Möbeln und Einrichtun-
gen, Ausstellungsgestaltungen | product designs
and furniture, exhibition designs (Kunsthalle
Krems, Galerie Engelhorn, Biennale Ljubljana)

Anton Schweighofer

geboren | born 1930 in Ayancik, Türkei | Turkey
Studium | education Akademie der bildenden
Künste Wien, Meisterklasse Clemens Holzmeister
(Diplom 1954) | Academy of Fine Arts Vienna under
Clemens Holzmeister (graduated in 1954)
Lehrtätigkeit | teaching 1977-1999 Professor für
Gebäudelehre und Entwerfen an der TU Wien |
Professor at TU Vienna

Werke | projects
Wohnbau Manteuffelstraße | Manteuffelstraße
housing complex Berlin; Stadtvillen Gatterburg-
gasse, Wien | Gatterburggasse villas, Vienna;
Vereinshaus Horn | Horn Club House; Stadtsaal
Mistelbach | Mistelbach community center; Kon-
rad-Lorenz-Institut, Wien | Vienna; Studentenheim,
Erlachplatz Wien | Erlachplatz student's dorm,
Vienna; Wohnbau Kaiser-Ebersdorf-Straße, Wien |
Kaiser-Ebersdrof-Straße housing complex, Vienna;
Geriatrie Franz-Josef-Spital, Wien | geriatrics care
center Franz-Josef-Hospital Vienna

Im Springer Verlag erschien 2000 die Monographie:
„Anton Schweighofer: Der stille Radikale" | publis-
hed by Springer in 2001: „Anton Schweighofer:
A Quiet Radical" (English edition)

Johannes Will
www.willl.at

geboren | born 1977
Studium | education Universität für angewandte
Kunst Wien | University of Applied Arts Vienna
(Diplom | graduated in 2002)

Werke | projects
WILLL Office; Single Lounge Vienna; Wind-
informationszentrum Prellenkirchen | Wind
Information Center Prellenkirchen (mit | with
Bernd Leopold)